Lily Tsoni has been writing for years but she made her debut as an author with "Josephine the white, the black, the yellow and the red" in Greek.

She has worked as a journalist and as a radio and TV producer and presenter (FM-1, 90FM, TRT, TV1, Star Channel), on programs about the Arts and Culture, the Child, Ecology, Health and, Travels throughout Europe.

She worked for the Agricultural Bank of Greece within the Directorates of Projects and Programming, International Relations and Transactions, and Inspection.

She attends courses in Classics at Cambridge University.
She has two kids.

By the same author:

- *Watch out the children, because... they don't abound!*
  (Greek title: Προσέξτε τα παιδιά γιατί... δεν μας περισσεύουν!)
- *Zozefina the black, the white, the yellow, and the red...*
  (Greek title: Η Ζοζεφίνα η μαύρη η άσπρη, η κίτρινη και η κόκκινη...)

LILY TSONI

Josephine
the black, the white...

Whenever I am in Lyon, I always dash to the second floor of Musée des Beaux-Arts to stand in front of Gericault Mad Woman's portrait. Last time, the guard of the museum looked at me strangely when he heard me calling her... "Maria!" Am I to blame that she is identical to poor Maria, Aristides' sister, of my childhood years?

Shhhhh!!! So, well Yes, I am Josephine the white, the black, the yellow and the red and I'm not kidding at all! Here are the organdies my mother used to sew for me; you can also ask Lela... Lelaaaaa!!! tell them!!!...

www.perfectpublishers.co.uk
e-mail: cambridgepen@yahoo.co.uk

First published in 2014 by Cambridge Pen Publishing House in collaboration with Perfect Publishers Ltd, Cambridge
Text © Lily Bartsioka-Tsoni 2014
The right of Lily Bartsioka-Tsoni to be indentified as the author of this work has been asserted.
All rights reserved. No part of this publication may be reproduced, stored in a retrieval system, or transmitted, in any form or by any means, electronic, mechanical, photocopying, recording or otherwise, without the prior permission of the author and Cambridge Pen Publishing House.

Title	Josephine the black, the white... Greek Literature
Author	Lily Tsoni
Translation	Lily Tsoni
Edited	Michele Spurdle Lily Tsoni
Illustration	Alexandra Christopoulou - De Palo Lily Tsoni
Copyright 2014	Lily Tsoni
UK Edition	March 2014, Publishing House Cambridge Pen in collaboration with Perfect Publishers Ltd, Cambridge
Edited by	Lily Tsoni & Publishing House Cambridge Pen

ISBN: 978-1-905399-98-7

What has been said about
« Josephine the black, the white... »

«[...] it is a very charming and evocative memoir...»

*Professor Richard Hunter,
Faculty of Classics at Cambridge University.*

«I read now your book and I must say that I love your writing very much.
It is delicate and lighthearted simultaneously. You have a lot of realistic elements but you attribute the emotions and characters with subtlety... it deserves to be read by as many readers as possible...»

*Pely Soussiopoulou,
Counsellor, Greek Embassy in Ottawa, Canada.*

«[...] I would say that you seriously have a gift for writing... Your choice of detail is good, your dialogue is life like, and (most important) the pace of narrative is swift and emotional...»

*Antony Verity,
Tutor of Classical Greek at Cambridge University
(Madingley Hall)*

[...] is fresh and successfully «maintains the immediacy of feeling».

*Modern Greek Language Association Awards,
Brunswick, USA*

DEDICATED to all children of the world, the white, the black... whatever their creed or culture... the children of today, as well as the children of yesterday and to those that will be born for as long as this planet is still turning...

Dedicated to the cute, little ghost of the innocence of childhood, which from time to time -though always uninvited- visits me, without ever scaring me at all...

and to the wild geese; Iksi and Kaksi, Kolmi and Neljä, Viisi and Kuusi, and to Morten the White male tame Goose, whose flock is always lead by the same leader, and this is Akka from Kebnekaise... Dedicated to Akka from Kebnekaise as well...

... heartfelt dedications also to my father Panagiotis, who was... the dad of Josephine...

LILY TSONI

CONTENTS LIST:

HOW I GREW UP...   10
(Looking through a small crack of the door, into Josephine's world.)

CHAPTERS:
1. ONCE, THERE WAS A FAMILY.   12
(Josephine's family roots.)
2. "*GRAMMAIRE ENFANTINE*" AND THE RAG-DOLL.   19
3. GRANDPA, MARIO'S FATHER.   27
(Josephine's grandpa and: the gypsies, Netos on his push-scooter, Achilles and his hoop, Simos on his long stilts, a young Japanese woman at cobbler shop and little Elenitsa eating a dragoon root.
4. THE LOOSE, WOOLEN, VERMILION LITTLE DRESS WITH THE WHITE, LACE COLLAR AND THE BLUE BOW.   46
(An accident that didn't happen.)
5. FLOWERS' "*COIFFURES*".   56
(That used to be Josephine's secret...)
6. A BOUQUET FOR HER MAJESTY.   65
(Queen Frederique visits the town.)
7. GOOD FOR THE "*AMERICANA*"!   70
(Joan the Americana in her new, Mary Quant Mini skirt and the two little poor sisters.)
8. LOOK AT THE BIRDIE!   82
(Bridegrooms from abroad.)
9. JOSEPHINE THE WHITE, THE BLACK...   91
(The bride was called Dominique and she was black.)
10. THE OLD WOMAN NAMED VOULA.   106
(She could make thin children be fatter!)
11. THE MUMPS.   118
(How old Voula used to... cure the mumps.)

Josephine

12. ARISTIDES AND MARIA.   125
(They never knew they were a symbol...)

13. PLACEMENT SERVICES FOR PERSONS THROUGH THE GREEK RED CROSS.   134
(Dr. Kakia met her family almost 40 years later.)

14. OUR VERY OWN SPY.   148
(A man of nowhere, who was going somewhere...)

15. THE GREEN-BOTTLE WITH THE STITCH.   155
(Children used to find ways to make their own toys...)

16. LITTLE KIKI, THE ONE WHO LEFT.   166
(Now she comes only in the dreams...)

17. GRANDMA.   181
(She was really brave and respectable and her favorite prayer was "*Ave Maria*" in Latin.)

AND I NO LONGER...   205
(So... yes, who knows... may be it's me *Josephine the White, the Black, the Yellow and the Red*; Josephine the friend of Akka from Kebnekaise... and I also used to be a close friend for years with Nils Holgersson as well as with Little Kiki and Elenenitsa, Achilles, Netos and Simos, Velissaris, Sotiria and Stathis; I was afraid of old Voula and Sorty Ourania; And I wish I had met my grandma who had the same name with me, my grandpa Nicolas as well as I wish all my favourites who left, were here; and... I miss my father...)

I WOULD NOW LIKE TO OFFER MY THANKS TO A NUMBER OF PEOPLE...   210
(Starting from Alexandra to the readers of the book...)

HOW I GREW UP...

I learnt to drive in the junk yard with the broken down, deserted cars next to my neighborhood. I pretended to be the driver and the engine and its horn simultaneously. And I'd stop pretending to be the driver, the engine and the horn until our spy had passed by us... and then I would continue until the grownups would call me home.

I learnt to dance, watching at the legs, the steps and the body's rhythm, at the parties I was taken by mom and dad; among cha-cha, the waltz, the twist and tango, the Charleston the shake and the blues.

Feeding dragonroot to Elenitsa, I learnt what friendship was all about, as she never ever held a drudge...

I forever lost Little Kiki and from her loss I've learnt, although I was still a child, what is like to lose somebody and to know that you'll never see them again, not even from afar...

They have taught me to love all the colors of the pallet and all the people. I grew up surrounded by love and imagination. Mom and Dad, Grandpa and Grandma, the whole town...

How I grew up...

And I'm being truthful when I say that, there were plenty of occasions until I grew up, that I helped Cinderella quickly sweep the cinders from the fireplace, while we searched time and again for her lost porcelain pump together, and when we couldn't find it, I'd comfort her sitting down beside her on her pumpkin carriage. Many were also the times when little and short, I had stood among the seven dwarfs without Snow-White getting wind of me.

Also there was more than a few times when, together with my daddy, we searched the forest for the bread crumbs so we could help Le Petit Poucet find his way back home.

And I would fall asleep in Grandpa's lap, in Grandma's arms, in mother's and Lela's and dream that the wild goose Akka from Kebnekaise had me on her wings... and I'd be awaken either by the sound the giant would make when I fell from the beanstalk and hit the ground or when I fell from the beanstalk and found myself with Alice in Wonderland, which finally, don't fool yourself, seemed not so very different to my land...

          Josephine

LILY TSONI

A CHILD, GENDER ♀. The blond baby with the green eyes wasn't brought by a stork. Nor was she found inside a cabbage in the garden. She was simply born, just like so many other babies in the world; in a private maternity clinic called "St. Helen". She grew up in the traditional way, listening to a whole world of fairytales, sometimes on her grandma or her grandpa's knees and sometimes in Augusta or Lela's lap. Later, she'd read Pollyanna[1], Lilika[2], Zil and Zacot[3] and she'd, of course, almost always fall asleep on the wings of Akka from Kebnekaise, the wild goose, flying with her and the rest of her flock, Yksi and Kaksi, Kolmi and Neljä, the male wild geese Viisi and Kuusi, and also Morten the White male tame Goose, on the wings of which Nils Holgersson[4] flew.

Augusta was her mother. She was about twenty-five, with brown hair and eyes. She was austerely beautiful. Her delicate manners and her outer elegance made up a personality that

---

[1] *Pollyanna (and the Glad Game)* 1913, by *Eleanor H. Porter*; the first of eleven more *Pollyanna* sequels.

[2] *Martine* (French, 1954), *Lilika* -that means *Little Lily*- (Greek), *Emma* (English); the little heroine of the *Martine Books*. A series of children's stories by *Gilbert Delahaye* and *Marcel Marlier*.

[3] *Jack* and *Jill* (1rst edition 1879) one of the many *"books for girls"* by *Louisa May Alcott*.

[4] From the *"Wonderfull adventures of Nils"* (1906, orig. *"Nils Holgerssons underbara genom Sverige"*; a geography reader for public schools, that made the Swedish author *Selma Ottilia Lovisa Lagerlöf* the first female author who win the Nobel Prize in Literature. Nils is still... flying on Morten the White male tame Goose's back on the reverse side of the Swedish 20 SK banknote while on the face side there is Selma Lagerlöf.

Once, a family...

dominated the surroundings positively, any surroundings she may have been in, without even trying.

Just as she knew how to behave, she also knew how to dress. Elegant Chanel suits, loose cloaks, stiletto heels. Low cleavages and open backs. Matching hats and shawls even matching shoes, bags, and gloves which were sometimes short and stopped sort of the wrists and sometimes long above the elbow. But also floral or polka dot, striped or checked balloon skirts. Overalls, blue jeans, chalopettes and jupe-culottes. Short loose manteaux and bows, buckles and suspenders and wide elastic hair ribbons, naval stripes tops and low-top, "Chucks" for walking...

A fine figure of a woman, with an adolescent face. A fresh, big filly, even under her conscientious and often expensive disguise...

Her father was Mario. A *distingué*[5]. A handsome young man, whose manners were impeccable, five years older than Augusta, raised in a northern village and self-made, he had proved through his hard work, ever since he was a twelve-year-old boy and apprentice, that he would go a long way. At the age of twenty-seven, he was running a fashion workroom, mainly for men but also for a few elective dressy and wealthy female customers who liked the fine, stylish and extra-vagant clothing; pantsuits, Le Smoking[6] tuxedo suits

---

[5] French in text: *distinguished*.
[6] *Le Smoking Tuxedo Suit*: A creation of *Yves St. Laurent (1966)*. A daring, mannish *trois-pieces* (French in text: *three piece*), chic, power pantsuit for women giving them the option to wear clothes that were normally worn only by men; it first earned attention in the popular culture in photographs by the fashion photographer Helmut Newton.

and mannish four piece suits; the fourth piece of which was the skirt.

He spent all six of his primary school years under the wing of the same and only teacher in the single-teacher primary school of his village. And beyond his not particularly pleasant and easy experiences of growing up during the occupation, meaning the German Occupation, the biggest advantage for him was his desire to improve his life; even as a child he would mould his future in his mind and dream of it. He earned his social status by means of his own achievements and built his prestige and reputation step by step.

In addition to this, Mario had undertaken an apprenticeship in the fashion world in Italy. This was due to circumstances that rather resembled a novel in the way they had come about and in the way they had turned out, under unexpected conditions and even more unexpected hospitality and friendship.

AN ITALIAN soldier, named Antonio, had been left behind wounded from the war in young Mario's village. The Italian hid for several days in the family's barn. He was wounded, hungry and exhausted. He was finally discovered one day by the dog of the house while chasing a chicken. The chicken had run and hidden in the barn and the dog had followed it. It was then that they understood why, in the past few days, they had been finding broken egg shells, especially behind the bales of clover in one of the corners of the barn. It seemed certain that the eggs he could easily find in the nests of the hens around there, and which he had eaten raw, had kept him alive, while he was in hiding: twenty six whole days! The unexpected visitor from the other side of the Adriatic sea tried to convey to them how many days he had been hiding himself, by

Once, a family...

counting on his fingers and repeating in Italian again and again... "uno, due, tre, quattro, cinque, sei, sette, otto, nove, dieci, undici, dodici, tredici, quattordici, quindici, sedici, diciasette, diciotto, dicianove, venti, ventuno, ventidue, ventitre, ventiquattro, venticinque, ventisei giorni!"[7] The suspicions, reservations and inhibitions were put aside in the first few moments after the surprise, as the family felt they had nothing to fear from a short, weak, bony and piteous little man, such as he was when they discovered him. They took care of him and nursed him, they gave him food and a bed so the Italian postponed leaving. Indeed, he helped them, in the family chores, in the fields and in the house. He learned rudimentary Greek and Mario did the same on his part, striving to learn Italian. In their free time, they'd go fishing in the river and would gallop with the horses. Antonio was a competent horse-rider and showed Mario various techniques.

Mario always remembered and laughed wholeheartedly at the time when Antonio was teaching him the secrets of horse riding. For some reason Mario's horse didn't obey him. It kept on galloping wildly and wouldn't stop no matter what. Then it scared the hell out of a donkey, which happened to be on the same path. There was an old woman, a villager, riding the donkey, together with two bundles of wood and a load of leaf mould. That poor donkey got so scared that it threw the old woman off. The leaf mould spilled and covered her. Mario, whose horse immediately stopped galloping and braced its

---

[7] Italian in text: *"one, two, three, four, five, six, seven, eight, nine, ten, eleven, twelve, thirteen, fourteen, fifteen, sixteen, seventeen, eighteen, nineteen, twenty, twenty one, twenty two, twenty three, twenty four, twenty five, twenty six days!"*

hooves after the old woman's fall, laughed uncontrollably instead of getting down from his horse to help the old woman. The old woman on the other hand, was trying to get up, in vain though because the donkey was firmly holding down her petticoat with one of its hooves. Confronted with the stubbornness of the donkey, with great difficulty and after a fair amount of time the old woman managed to free herself from the animal's hold, tearing her petticoat. As soon as she got to her feet, she started beating the donkey with hands and feet, cursing it at the same time. Then, she started chasing, not the dumb creature which had fled braying after her kicks, but Mario who in the meantime had jumped off his horse and continued laughing his head off and holding his stomach. Antonio had arrived right on time, hitting his mare with the horsewhip and screaming orders in Italian, in his attempt to reach Mario who could have been in danger, such was the way that he had bolted on a horse which galloped madly. It was Antonio who had saved him that day from the rage of the furious woman who hit Mario anywhere she could reach with her hands and with a broken stick that happened to be there. She pulled his hair and yelled that she would tear it out even though Mario was sure that this would be the case even if the old woman hadn't clarified her intentions. And Antonio may have saved Mario, but he too got a beating and suffered dearly till he tore himself away from her hands. Antonio had been shouting *"strega, strega!"*, which means *"witch"*, *"sibyl"*, or something similar. The old woman thought that he was telling her *"steka, steka!"* which meant *"hold on"* for the people in the village and she'd replied *"No, you stupid Italian, I won't hold on! I'll beat you till you're dead!"* And she'd bent over for rocks which she'd hurled at both of them. They'd covered their heads with their hands and jumped around to save

Once, a family...

themselves from the stoning. In the end, it was the Hayward who had saved both of them from "death by stoning" which the old woman had condemned them to.

Many more small incidents, most of them funny, had bonded Mario and Antonio. For Mario, it was as if he had suddenly gained an older brother, and wonderfully one that neither beat him nor made fun of him if he did something dumb. A brother, who had suddenly popped out of nowhere in order to protect him. Brothers, who may not have understood completely what the other would say, but nevertheless, seemed to communicate just fine and that was something that Mario had never managed with his older brother Stephan even though they spoke the same language. When finally, after two to three years or so, Antonio made the decision to return to Italy, everyone was dumbfounded. When the time also came to say goodbye, everyone in the house was crying. Moreover, everyone in the village had come to love Antonio and there were many eyes watering when they informed that *"the Italian is leaving."*

Antonio left for his country because his people were waiting for him. As he had promised Mario, he didn't forget him. Their friendship continued even when Antonio crossed the Adriatic. He would send post-cards and Mario would show them to his fellow-villagers in the village coffee house in the evening. *"Thez iz "TRULLI" -very nais house. Good winder all!"* (these are traditional "dome" (TRULLI) houses. A good winter to everyone). *"Meny Hapy Reterns. Hapy Neo Year all!"* (Many Happy Returns. A Happy New Year to everyone!) Antonio tried to write in Greek. In cute, funny, broken (multi-broken to be exact!) Greek, and everyone in the village gloated that the Italian respected their language and was also learning it. It was to Antonio, thus, that Mario owed his trip to Italy, where for three whole years he had offered him exactly what he needed; a great training by the side of an Italian dressmaker.

SHE WAS BAPTIZED Josephine. She was named after her father's mother. A grandma that never got the chance to hold her on her knees. This Italian-like name was owed to grandmother's Roman godmother, Donna Lucia.
A godmother that everyone talked about but no one had ever met. Not even grandma, because as it was said, after grandma's christening, her godmother had left for her country and never came back to Greece. However, it was also said that she never forgot her godchild and Donna Lucia proved this literally and stopped proving it only when she died. Only then did the postman stop bringing parcels with brand-new clothes in flamboyant fabrics, sewn in European style and European design, and a whole bunch of little things and trinkets, enviable as well as bizarre and actually not only in the eyes of the Greek village of those times since not even in the towns did the women wear such things. They looked more like clothes and accessories for showgirls and that's why grandma had most of them tucked away in her chest without ever using them.
"The first girl born who will take my name will also take these. If none of you bears a female, then divide it among your wives", such was it reported that Mario's mother, grandma Josephine, had said to her two sons.
So, Mario and Augusta's daughter got Grandma Josephine's name and together with that she inherited that huge chest filled with clothes and trinkets that grandmother's godmother, Donna Lucia, had been sending for years and years.

Chapter 2   "Grammaire Enfantine"

THE WALLS of the groud floor, just as the rest of the house, were painted ivory and blue. The floor was wooden, made of huge floor-boards. The right wall was the *wall of portraits* as Galatia, Augusta's sister, called it. There, on a huge oval wooden frame, was a portrait of Augusta's parents. In the portrait next to it, the little girl with the pretty eyes and her hair in two thick braids was grandmother, Augusta's mother and next to that, the little boy was grandmother's brother, Nicolas. Another portrait of Nicolas on his graduation day from the French university he attended and right next to that, a portrait of Mario's parents, which Augusta had arranged to have done, by giving a painter the only photograph his parents had had taken together. There was even a portrait of Augusta and one of Mario, while the most recent was that of Josephina on her second birthday. Frames in different shapes and sizes in wood, stannous, silver and German silver, contained pictures of all the members of the family and stood out against the white wall where the portraits ended. It was a very beautiful and nostalgic wall, full of memories and love.

The dining room created a remarkable impression: a huge commode with drawers and cupboards, big and small and a credenza with an oval mirror between two sconces, while the table was very long with fourteen chairs all around it and two silver flambeaus. It resembled those tables in the monasteries at which the monks all sit around to eat, although it also looked like the tables in barracks. It was a heavy handmade construction made of walnut. Augusta's father had made it with his bare hands a short time before he was sent to exile and so stopped working. It had been an order placed by an English doctor who had come and settled in Greece because he was a lover of ancient Greek history. He cited Homer as if he had written it himself. He loved the ancient Greek theatre and knew all Greek history by heart. He had left suddenly though, following his heart which in turn followed his Italian missionary friend Patricia, somewhere in Africa.

His furniture, all of which was handmade and tasteful, was more or less given to Augusta who at that time was building her home and preparing her wedding. Some pieces of furniture had been brought from England; the rest had enormous sentimental value for Augusta since her father had made them.

ON THAT SAME dining table, Josephina tried on the clothes that Augusta made for her, sometimes alone and sometimes with the help of Constantia who also had a little girl of the same age, little Kiki. At other times, because Mario hardly ever had time, he'd ask for the help of the seamstress. And even though Augusta had never sat with a seamstress to learn the art of dress-making, she managed well. She'd do the designing, cut the fabric, put the pieces together, have fittings and reach the stage of sewing; meaning, that she stopped right before the sewing. She stopped there. She didn't know how to sew and she would never learn. Whatever she set her mind on doing, she did it, just as whenever she set her mind on not being able to do something, she never did. That's how it had happened with sewing. She simply said that she'd never learn how and she didn't. Even though she had bought two sewing machines, a *Pfaff* with a foot pedal and a *Singer* with manual movement, she never used either of them. This is the part where she was helped either by the seamstress or Constantia. Accordingly the long dining table would be

Chapter 2   "Grammaire Enfantine"

baptized as a *catwalk* for the purpose of these moments.

Augusta's favourite fabric, which she liked creating garments with for her daughter, was organdie. For her it was the fabric of dreams. Organdies in pink, rose, snow white, ciel, vert amande[8] and yellow.

In pastel tones; the tones of clouds and dreams. With the manufacturer's names -European usually- on their selvage.

Unwrapping the bolts of organdies which the shop assistants took down from their shelves, was a game for her.

A tuck at the waist, puffy sleeves or none at all, a waistband that wrapped around the waist and tied in the back with a huge bow. Organdies, some waisted and fluffy, some baggy and loose with huge or baby collars and a hornet-nest or plaits in the bodice. Josephina would turn left and right whenever she was asked, tirelessly and without complaining.

She'd lift her little hands up high, she'd spread them out sideways, depending on the needs of the fitting. Sometimes she'd let out a small, stifled cry whenever she got pricked. Organdie without a farthingale didn't exist, at least not for Augusta. It was worn underneath as a petticoat. It was white or see-through, cotton or linen. Its success assured the success of the organdie; while the farthingale's own success was assured by a good starching. The laundry starch was a white, thick powder in white tiny plastic galipots in the size of an inkbottle in the compressed shape of the earth, with horizontal lines. After the farthingale had soaked in the starch

---

[8] French in text: *the pastel colour of the green almond.*

for some time it was then ironed moist. It then looked like paper; it was very erect and set the organdie off to advantage when worn underneath.

BETWEEN the dining room and the living room with the deep blue English sofas, above the armchairs with the golden patina and the gobelin tapestry, there was a wooden, Edwardian doll's house from the English doctor's doll collection. He had left before he had the chance to complete his collection and so there was plenty of room for Augusta to put her own dolls up there. Dolls with hair drawn as curls, porcelain dolls, but also plastic ones of hard or soft material, with cloth bodies too, and dolls with fake hair that looked real. The hostess took good care of all of them, personally.

She'd dust them herself, she'd wash and comb their hair, and she'd laundered their clothes. Once a year, usually after summer, she'd place all of them naked in the tub so the dust of summer would be washed away. She'd take care of them as if they were real babies. What Lela didn't understand, however, was why one of them was seated on top of a red foreign book when there were two bookcases inside the house. Once or twice, to tell the truth, she had attempted to take it from there and put it somewhere on the bookcase. Augusta had told her "*Put it back in its place, please*" and "*don't ever move it from there, please*" and Lela had remained with the unanswered question "*What business has a book up there?*" Augusta, even though she had the explanation ready, didn't want to be melodramatic in front of Lela, who, she could already imagine, would start crying her heart out if she heard it.

SO SHE KEPT the answer for when her daughter had grown up a little more and would also ask her, "*What is a book doing*

Chapter 2   "Grammaire Enfantine"

in the doll house?" She'd tell her something like this...

"Josephina, you know that as a child I didn't have dolls... On just one occasion, my godmother gave me a doll one Easter. My happiness, however, didn't last long, only five to ten minutes, for as long as I held her in my arms... You see, I didn't have time to enjoy it, to become her mother, to rock her to sleep in my arms, to bathe her and comb her hair even if she had fake drawn hair on her head that couldn't be combed... I didn't have time to do any of these things. My godmother's daughter grabbed her from my hands, crying and shouting that she wanted it for herself. My godmother, who never denied any of her indulgences, preferred to give it to her. She told me that she'd give it back to me later. She never did...

There was another time that I came really close to becoming a real doll-mom. It was the time that I had collected money from the carol of Lazarus...

I remember going from door to door with my girlfriends, the whole neighborhood, singing the Lazarus. You know... 'Lazarus came, the bay leaves came...' We'd each hold a little basket adorned with flowers. April flowers and anemones, violets and daffodils, roses and Madonna Lilies. Around noon, I counted all the money I had collected. Halfpennies, even pennies, a couple of two pence and a ten pence! Let alone that my godmother had given me a whole twenty drachmas! At last! I was going to buy a doll! The money was enough! I would at last have a doll and one that would be bought from my own earnings. I ran to your grandmother to tell her... I even knew which doll I was going to buy. I had chosen her days before. I would buy her and none other. The one with the pink sponge dress. I had picked her out from among the rest on the wooden shelf of the toy store. I had even talked to her even though she was behind the shop window! I had promised her that I would buy her, that I would become her mom.... It seemed to me that she smiled at me every time I told her because I told her every day! I'd be there every day! Daily! Outside the shop window. I had even counted the freckles she had on her cheeks. She had eight freckles on her right cheek and seven on the left... Unfortunately, nothing happened then, either... Your grandmother took the money I had collected. She had always been a very practical person. She bought me that red book for when I went to high school. I would have to start French then and as Mademoiselle Mari, who lived next to us, had advised her, I'd need two or three good books which couldn't be easily found and cost a lot of money.

"You'll need this in two years time from now, in high school" she had said.

"In two years time? From now for the year after next? But we have time for two years from now! I will sing again and I'll buy the book! Where will I find the doll again?"

She did it; she bought the book. Some pennies were left over. She bought me a pair of white bobby socks. These, she had

Chapter 2   "Grammaire Enfantine"

told me, were far more useful and essential than a doll whose her head, arms and legs would eventually fall off! I, of course, insisted that nothing would fall off! Neither her head nor her arms nor her legs! I wouldn't let anything fall off! I'd watch her like a hawk! I didn't succeed in persuading her.

I never passed by that shop window again, except for one afternoon. A little while before the shops opened. I had to explain to the doll why I wouldn't be buying her. I didn't want her to think that I had been fooling her all that time... I don't know if she believed me. I think her little face grew dark. I am sure it did... Surely she got upset. She was looking at me while I was in tears, explaining.

Then... then I never went by there again... I shied away from the toy shop for more than a year... When I found myself again outside its shop window, because it was on my way and I couldn't do much about it, the doll didn't exist. I was suddenly glad that my favorite doll left the window and now be living among a family. Before that day, I had been praying for a long time that some other child would buy her. A child that would love her and who wouldn't let her head come off nor her arms nor her legs. I had been praying that she would love her at least as much as I had loved her...

As for me, I had already returned to my rag dolls that the grown-ups made for me. And I'd imagine that they were real dolls that had a head and mouth and arms and legs, even fingers. That's how my longing for a real doll would ease a little bit. The dream, though, wouldn't die. One day I'd acquire a regular doll... A Real Doll... and I... I would then become a real doll-mom... So, this is why I have "Le Grammaire Enfantine"⁹ here, among the dolls... because this book could have been my first doll..."

---
[9] French in text: *"Grammar for Children"*, by *Claude Augé* (*LAROUSSE*, 1rst edition 1900, Paris).

Chapter 3   Grandpa, Mario's father.

HE WAS BORN in summer, on the wheat field his father was reaping with his scythe. His mother was tying them up in bundles with her belly in her mouth. That's where the labour pains started. She gave birth and cut the cord off all by herself under a fir tree. Either way she didn't have enough time to head back for the village. She wrapped him in her arms with the clothes she had been wearing. Then she called out to her husband, who continued to reap and hadn't got wind of what had happened, and she showed him his son.

HE WAS tall, about 1,80 and lofty. "He has the body of a statue!" Lela used to say. He also had beautiful, bright light blue eyes. Augusta said that she had come across this colour in a handmade murano[10], nowhere else. Lela insisted that she had seen it in the glass marbles that children played with. He was almost ninety but he looked at least fifteen years younger.

"Grandpa, what kind of old age is this?" "You have all your marbles!" She often admired.

He lived alternatively, one year with Mario and his family and one year with his other son, Stefanos. All his life seemed to fit inside two suitcases. Among other things, a white and brown picture of his wife. As soon as he arrived, he would place the brownish picture on his bed-side table and would yell at Lela if she moved it an inch while dusting.

---

[10] Italian in text: Famous glass, exclusive product of the small *island of Murano* in the *Laguna Veneziana* (Venetian Lagoon).These glassmakers were the most prominent citizens of the island and before the end of the 16th century they were not allowed to leave the Venetian Republic.

"Do you know what this picture is to me? It is my whole my life!"

He liked to embrace loudly, from deep within his soul, all those things that he knew would never be again. Lela and Josephina were his loyal audience. They never got bored by his nostalgic narratives even though he often said the same things over and over. He narrated so prettily, stopping at tiny little details.

It was always a sweet, warm and tender narration. Grandfather tidied up his memories by doing this, which was why they never got forgotten in the rust of time. For Josephina it was like a fairytale with a lot of chapters.

"*Grandpa,* this is your favorite fairytale, isn't it?" she had asked him.

He was also unpredictable, in his own contradictions. An intense personality, with a quality which was easily distinguished and never forgotten. A local hillbilly, a typically uneducated man who had only attended the three first grades of primary school, yet impressed everyone with his knowledge and spirit because he was, in essence, educated. He talked and read.

He read and made notes. Grandfather had even read Homer, quiet apart from all the knowledge he had about the rest of the ancient times. At the Acropolis, he managed the tour better than a tour guide as he regularly kept company with a History Professor, an old Athenian.

"When I first heard Before Christ this and After Christ that I got confused! And I said to myself that I have to learn! It seemed like a great deal! I got down and studied History! It

Chapter 3   Grandpa, Mario's father.

didn't take much to learn it!" Grandfather explained.

At one time when Mitsi, Augusta's younger sister, escorted her Danish friend, Birth, and her family to the Acropolis, they couldn't find a tour guide available and grandfather had managed pretty well. Even the tour guide of the other group had congratulated him as he happened to be listening. Grandpa also did very well in Geography, mainly cultural geography. He was a *"wonder-gramps"*, as everyone who knew him said.

He always went to Sunday Mass and kept a fast scholastically all his life. On Wednesdays, Fridays and on all the Church fasting days. And during Lent, he kept a fast for all the days. All forty of them. He didn't even eat olive oil.

On one particular afternoon the spaghetti didn't seem to be only water boiled. There was something wrong with it. On his second bite, he asked Lela if she had added oil on them.

"No! Oil? Me? Given that you eat your food without olive oil grandpa I just added a little butter so you don't get ill with all this oiless food for forty days!" she started to soothe him. Mario and Augusta looked at each other and almost choked with laughter. Grandpa turned red.

"You have made me sin! The devil put you up to it and you made me sin! Butter! Since I don't eat olive oil? Dear me! Where does butter come from? Isn't it made of milk? Isn't milk a sin? What have you done to me! How will you raise a family in the future if you can't tell the difference between oil and butter?" He yelled at her wagging his fork.

"Calm down grandpa, you'll poke my eye out!" she retorted

in fear *"Why is butter bad?"* Josephina asked but nobody was listening to her. Lela told him that she'd take the sin on herself but grandpa wouldn't accept it.

"What do you want, then? You want me to hang myself because I've made a mistake? Tell me, is that what you want? Haven't you ever made a mistake?"

"I have, of course I have!" Grandpa admitted and finally cooled off and forgave her.

"That's why I love you Grandpa and respect you! Because you're honest!"

TWO NEIGHBORHOOD children, Achilles and Simos, also loved grandpa, each for their own reasons.
"The Gypsies are coming!" the children shouted with the same happiness that they'd shout *"the swallows are coming!"* They were coming to the fields, there, where the town ended and the children from other neighborhoods, further away would follow the caravan to the place they would camp. They'd jump around the wagons and the gypsy women would smile. The gypsy men were more dismal; they had thick, black mustaches and a whip in hand. They'd jump off their wagons and set up their cloth houses in no time. The gypsy children would get in their way and they would scold them.
The children were usually bare foot and half naked. They were also usually dirty from the dirt of the journey. Some pieces of dirt would shine on their skin. Their hair was messy and uncombed. Tangled and dull. Their eyes were shiny like the beads they wore on their necks, their hands and their legs. Big and expressive, impressing and cunning, whatever color they may have been. Then, they'd gather dried twigs and hay

Chapter 3   Grandpa, Mario's father.

from the freshly harvested fields and light fires outside each tent for the pots they would heat water in, in order to bathe their children.

The children dried their hair before the heat of the fire and each family would eat sitting on the ground around the fire, where after the baths, they'd place the cauldrons for their food. The smell that surged from the cauldrons was odd and heavy. The children of the neighbourhood wrinkled their noses but didn't seem to be able to tear themselves away. Spaghetti with red sauce which smelled intensely of pork grease and the porcupine in the red sauce was the most common gypsy dinner.

NETOS came with a group of boys from the other side of town, on their kick scooters. They were going to play tag and would try to exchange a broken, fallen apart toy or some weird item that the gypsy children would have to hand. They would reestablish friendships and would know all each other's names by heart. They would try to understand their dialect and the gypsy children would try to teach it to  them. While at the celebration of the gypsy wedding, they always became the best of friends and the gypsy women never sent their children to bed early. Everything was more permissive. Even the faces radiated oddly and glowed in the fires. Their eyes sparkled with less cunningness. The gold and the silver and the beads they wore on the hands, legs and feet, old and young alike, men and women, made strange reflections and took on weird colors. Those ornaments blended in with that bridal night.

ACHILLES had come rolling his large hoop, using its stick with a lot of virtuosity and holding in his other hand a slice of bread with grape cream. He asked when the wedding was going to take place. They told him that it had already taken place that afternoon. They also showed him the bridal tent. He glimpsed inside through the opening of the tent door.

The bride and the groom were sitting cross-legged, discreet and mute. The groom would give the children, who crowded outside to see them, a smile now and again. The bride was crouched. Two or three old women were also sitting on the floor cross legged opposite the groom. They were also mute. All around them the dowry was stacked in small piles. Blankets and rugs, carpets and looms. Everything in that tent was mute and seemed sorrowful even though it was a day of joy.

I complete contrast, outside the tent there was a big feast going on. A bridal celebration. Gypsy men were drinking arrack and clutching their tin cups, talking loudly and ordering their women and children around. Gypsy girls were cackling and peeping at the rest. Gypsy women were talking loudly and stirring the food which boiled inside the cauldrons with tin ladles. Meat in red sauce and spaghetti. The gypsy children were yowling while playing or tumbling around and falling, letting out the same cries in both cases. The older

Chapter 3 Grandpa, Mario's father.

gypsies, the more stricken in years, would sing now and again. They'd sing strange sad songs, also dipped in melancholy, and would shut their eyes as if they were in pain.

An old gypsy man, the oldest, beat on a tambourine. Five or six gypsy girls danced slowly and sensually. The children were laughing loudly and the men got nasty. They pushed them aside from the bridal tent but they continued to laugh loudly and so the men gesturing, told them to leave. They didn't budge an inch. They were standing behind the gypsies who were sitting on the ground and then the men started playing tag with their kids.

Netos had told them to leave. To be exact, he had said, *"Busters, vanish, it's time to go! My mom will beat me silly again tonight..."* That's how Netos always talked. Even though Achilles -the younger of all!!- was the leader, Netos was something like the second in command and he had taken on the issues of order in the gang. Achilles however, wanted them to remain... And he was the leader! He took his iron wheel again and rolled it to the newlyweds' tent. For some reason many gypsies were crowding around the opening of the door, alongside the curious people from the neighborhood who had come. The child leaned so that he could see between the crowds. He couldn't. He stood on his toes. Not even then could he see anything. He went to the side. He fell with his belly on the ground. He lifted the cloth between the pegs where they tied the stretched ends of the tent. It was enough for him to get his head through and see what was going on inside. He wormed his way quickly half inside the tent. His upper body was inside and his lower body outside the tent. The rest of the gang kneeled around him and pulled his legs and shirt, asking him to come out so they too could have a look.

The first one who got wind of him was the groom. He laughed and showed him to the bride. She turned, looked, and then resumed her hunched position like a *speechless, motionless, good little soldier*... The two gypsy women, who continued to sit opposite the groom in silence, stood up and started shouting in their language, pointing at Achilles.

Like a flash, the gypsy men who were sitting drinking arrack, gathered around the tent. One of them grabbed Achilles by the legs after he had angrily pushed the children aside. However, at the same time, the two old women were pulling him inside by the armpits. For several seconds, Achilles was going back and forth, inside and out of the tent. The groom continued to laugh. Finally and fortunately for Achilles the *insiders* managed to reach an agreement with the *outsiders*. The outsiders let go of his legs and the child was pulled inside by the old woman. He managed to get a fleeting glimpse of the interior and the bride before the old women who were still holding him by the armpits, shoved him outside.

One of the gypsy men, who earlier on had wanted to break his iron-wheel, as it had almost fallen into one of the cauldrons, grabbed him with dander by the shoulder sleeves of his white cotton shirt and drew him close to the cauldrons with the thick, red sauce and spaghetti. He dipped his hand inside a copper pan. When he took it out, he stroked the hapless Achilles on the head. He was spreading something on his hair as he stroked him... The rest of the gypsies laughed. The women objected to what the man was doing and showed it... The girls cackled and urged him to go on. The man agreed. He was continuously spreading that something, which looked

Chapter 3   Grandpa, Mario's father.

slithery, on the child's hair, flatting it out with his palms, making it shine in the light of the fires. After he had basted him well, he pointed with his finger, the way to leave.

Achilles, who was on the verge of blowing up but didn't dare speak out, felt relieved. They set off, with him leading the way. He was in front and the rest followed. Netos helped him with his iron-wheel. On the way, they'd lean over their leader's head, which looked smothered; they'd smell it, make faces and burst into laughter. He'd then kick them on the shins and touch his hair. He could smell that *something* that the gypsy had spread on him and then he'd wipe that *something* off on his clothes. It smelled like something between cod-liver oil, which his mother fed him, and grease and fried butter. It was awful. On the way, they met Josephine's grandfather.

"Where are you young rascals wandering at this time of night?" he had asked and they explained. He leaned over and smelled his head, too.

"Hell, this thing here is burned and strained pork grease!" he adjudicated immediately.

"Gramps, come home with me so that my ma won't give me a beating!" the defeated leader begged grandpa and he agreed.

"Grandpa, what have they done to you? What have they done? I'll hang them!" The mother screamed and attacked Achilles. He started running round and round the yard table and she chased him, holding a rod she had handy for such occasions.

The kid was shouting: *"Help, gramps!"* and grandpa shouted

in vain that her son had done nothing to him. She couldn't hear a thing! He got between them, putting himself at risk of getting the beating the mother was intending for her son. Suddenly the game of chase ended abruptly. At the moment Achilles escaped a beating.

"But, I thought you had come here to complain! However, he is still getting a beating!" the mother retorted and prepared to recommence her chase. Achilles held on to grandpa's trousers and jumped to the left and right, hiding behind him.

His mother, firstly because she was very much embarrassed to chase her son around grandpa, and secondly because she saw that she wouldn't succeed in catching him, ceased chasing for a second time.

"Don't beat him tonight! Tonight, all he needs is a good bath! Do you know how pork grease smells in this heat?"

The pork grease, that slimy thing that was mired on her child's head wouldn't come off no matter what! She gave him a haircut as best as she could to get through the night and in the morning, she took him to the barber's and he cut all his hair off! He was scalped!

"Gramps, thanks. You saved me from a beating! Whatever you need, I'm here!" Achilles made this significant statement a few days later, placing his hand on his chest.

"Thank you, but... I hope you'll be unneeded!" Grandpa retorted with laughter.

Chapter 3   Grandpa, Mario's father.

"I want you to know, that from that night on, I also say my prayers for you!" he added softly, so the rest wouldn't hear him and make fun of the fact that a tough leader had such sensitivities.

SIMOS, the small neighbor, came walking on stilts. He was huge, he walked slowly and carefully and everyone stared at him in awe, asking him what it was like up there. He'd burst with pride, wouldn't give a satisfying answer and made them envy him. Like a real star of his kind, he left questions unanswered. He never revealed where he had found the stilts, who had made them for him, who had given them to him or how he had learnt to walk on them. Neither did he reveal whether he had had a hard time learning or if it had taken him long.

He would smile enigmatically and make his next slow but sure and correct lope, looking at them mischievously, literally from *above*.

The little guys crowded around the stilts and Simos was on the verge of losing his balance. He asked them to step aside, not to cling on to the stilts because he'd fall. They didn't obey. Grandpa was sitting on a bench rolling tobacco on a white piece of paper. This is what he always did every afternoon after lunch. He'd secretly smoke a cigarette because Mario had forbidden him to smoke. Mario was concerned about his father and would treat him as if he were the child and Mario the father. Simos continued to plead louder this time, feeling more indignant. As he opened both hands, spreading them out wide, the misfortune wasn't far from happening. Simos' body tilted once to the right and once to the left then to the right again and finally slanted far forward. The stilts got tangled, the child was about to fall and the little ones simultaneously let out an identical cry of horror. However, the misfortune didn't happen, because grandpa, who had already detected that something was wrong, kept throwing glances at Simos and the bunch that surrounded him. He abruptly and hurriedly jumped up and ran towards the children. He caught Simos in mid air before he fell on the children, thus injuring them and himself. The cloth-cap fell from grandpa's head and his glasses broke into pieces. The result of the damage found Simos with a sprained leg because one of the stilts didn't jerk off like it should have while he was falling but continued to be tied to his leg. Fortunately, among all those children, only one got hurt lightly on the head, acquiring a lump. Afterwards, grandpa escorted him, or to be more exact, he carried the small injured Simos home. The bunch of children, the same bunch that a while ago had made Simos fall, followed them. And so Simos, from that day on, whenever he saw grandpa, would run to say *"thank you"* as if it were the first time he was seeing him after the accident. Moreover, he'd always say:

"Grandpa, you're in my heart, I want you to know that!" and grandpa would answer with a smile: *"I know, I know, you be careful now!"*

THE NEWS travelled fast. All news travels fast. Anestis, the man who owned the grill house at the corner, had a son who was a radio operator on the ships. Now he was returning the following week, bringing a Japanese woman with him.

"Japanese? With a pillow in the back and knitting pins in the hair?"

Chapter 3   Grandpa, Mario's father.

Questions and discontent, as if the Japanese girl the young spark was bringing with him, belonged to the whole neighborhood.

"How will she get around with the pillow in the back and the knitting pins in the hair?"

The questions and descriptions of those who were supposedly knowledgeable about 'things' reached the ears of Anestis' wife, Mrs. Poppy. She, in turn, threw fits saying that she wouldn't allow her daughter-in-law to go about with knitting pins in her hair so as not to poke anyone's eyes out every time she'd turned her head or with a pillow on her back so as not to make a fool of herself and the family.

"Pins are for knitting and not for the hair! And pillows are for sleeping on and not for carrying around here and there!"

Grandpa, as he always did, passed by Anagnou's cobbler's shop -which smelt of glue and leather- to say good morning. The cobbler was spiking a beetle-crusher, taking cover behind a small pile of mixed up shoes which dwelt on his wooden work-bench. Behind him was an even bigger pile of shoes. Each time they'd bring in a shoe for repair, he'd throw it over his right shoulder and it assumed its position on the hill of eternal shoes, since most of them remained there for years.

"My daughter-in-law, Augusta, has a Japanese friend in Athens, a real Japanese, a very good girl, her name is Keiko and she doesn't wear any of those things, neither pillows on her back nor knitting pins in her hair!" he tried to explain to

Costas and his customers who numbered about half a dozen and who were standing around trying to find a solution to the *problem*, as if the Japanese girl were to come to their homes with or without knitting pins in the hair and a pillow on the back; it didn't matter either way. He didn't succeed in convincing them.

"You don't know what you're talking about!" they told him.

All of them believed the same thing: *"The Japanese, the real Japanese women, wear knitting pins in their hair and a pillow on their back!"*

Suddenly, they all crowded around the window at the shoe store entrance. The cobbler stood up, shoved his beetle-crusher inside the pocket of his apron, pushed them aside and assumed first stage seat. Manolis, the spark who had returned, crossed the street and was heading their way and a young Japanese girl -at least that's what her eyes conveyed- was holding him by the arm. They entered the shoe shop. How beautiful she was! A real stunner!

"Glad... glad to meet you, my girl! Anagnou! Constantine Anagnou!" the cobbler introduced himself formally, kissing her hand after he had wiped his hands on his apron. The rest were leaning over her back in order to see the notorious pillow. Nothing. No pillow. They looked at her hair. No knitting pins, nowhere. It turned out that grandpa was right. They were disappointed. They had prepared themselves for something exotic and strange and this Japanese girl here, who for days now had been causing a flutter in the quiet city, looked real... and she must have been, but her attire was exactly the same as their women! The only difference was her eyes. Beautiful, black, almond shaped.

Chapter 3   Grandpa, Mario's father.

"This here, my men, is Keiko!" Manolis was heard saying and all of them turned to stare at grandpa who just a short while ago had been telling them about Augusta's friend, the Japanese whose name was also Keiko. Good going grandpa! "But, I'm not sure... are all Japanese women called... *Keiko?*" they wondered...

ELENITSA was sweet and cute. And stone-pelting was her favorite habit. Josephine always cheated and Elenitsa wouldn't put up with that; she'd get angry and leave. She'd go up the ridge beside the railroad tracks, lift white jagged stones and sling them with fury at Josephine's yard and house. She'd chuck stones until her hands were sore. The war was conducted with solitary ammunition, that of Elenitsa. Every time, until that small guerilla declared a cease fire, no one dared to venture out of Josephina's house. Once, when Lela had dared, a rock had hit her on the ankle.

Morfoula, the mother of the little one, would raise her hands in despair˙ *"I scold her, of course I scold her! What? Do you think I praise her? She's a small child though, what should I do with her?"*

The truth was that Elenitsa needed a good spanking but who was to give it to her? Apart from her stone-pelting wars, she was amiable and innocent. Augusta never held a grudge and Josephina never stopped loving her. The very next day, after the stone-pelting wars, Elenitsa would show up again and ask, as if nothing had happened, *"Shall I come and play?"*

Augusta would accept her and tried each time to analyze in depth the causes and occasions of the recent war so that she could set her right. Anyway, she was considered part of the family and they had gotten used to her whims.

"Why do you bother taking her in? She'll crack your heads open one of these days, let alone that we too are also in danger!" the neighbors would tell Augusta. Augusta, however, believed that Elenitsa would become the best of them all.

"You'll see!" She'd say with certainty and they'd just shake their heads and add *"I'll have to see that to believe it"*, *"good grief!"* and other such comments.

IT WAS almost noon. The two girls had climbed the common garden wall on the side of Mrs. Veneko's garden. Thought they were enjoying their *cockerel* lollipops, they parted with their little hands as best as they could the plants that were clinging there so that they could see better through the fence. Mrs. Veneko's garden... A garden full of broad beans. Many broad beans, erect like little soldiers mustered in straight lines with their black and white flecked flowers which gave the appearance of faces. The faces of soldiers. Josephina wouldn't have it any other way! That's the way it was! They were little soldiers, she persisted in explaining to disbelieving Elenitsa. Josephina always began her day with *"the children of Aunt Lena"*[11] on the radio, and often during lunch, when they ate together, Lela ,would read a story to her whereas at

---

[11] *"Child's hour"* used to be the most wide children's radio programme (by the Greek National Radio) during the 50's and 60's. Thousands of the today adults grew up listening every day to *Auntie Lena's* (*Antigone Metaxa*) fairytales and songs and used to do their morning workout in front of the radio of the family following to her commands. Now she has gone; grew ups do always remember her tenderly...

Chapter 3   Grandpa, Mario's father.

night she'd always fall asleep, listening to one from Augusta, grandpa or Lela. Her imagination was very vivid and her descriptions persuasive. Elenitsa would listen to her in fear.

"... *they're soldiers I tell you! Yes! And Alice in the Wonderland, wasn't she chased by soldier-cards? Remember? Don't be astonished if these broad beans here become soldiers suddenly too! Look at how they're looking at us! See? Look at how they're standing! To attention! Just like soldiers!*" And she stood up beside the iron fence with her legs joined, her chest out and tummy in, her hands straight and parallel to her body and her head upright and motionless. "*Maybe they're spell-bound, too! They could be real soldiers who have had a spell cast on them by the bad witch! Like the frog-prince! You do remember the frog-prince, don't you?*"

"*I remember him!*" Elenitsa was now very frightened.

"*I think that someday, these ones here will become real soldiers again! When the magic spell is broken! Then they'll stop being broad beans! You'll see!*" Josephina said meaningfully.

"*And what if... what if all these broad beans turn into real soldiers and start stone... pelting us?*" Elenitsa mumbled, her eyes wide open. She jumped down the common wall and started running towards the gate of the garden, scared silly at the thought that a, whole army of broad beans could rise in insurrection any minute now and start chasing them, pelting them with stones. She tripped and fell. The thorns of the pink rose bush got caught in her dress. She yanked it. It tore. She shook off the freshly watered earth from her clothes but it didn't come off. Josephine helped clean off the greenery of the moss which was growing between the stones... that didn't come off either.

A strange looking plant that stood upright among its big leaves caught Elenitsa's eye. It was orange, yellow and red. With a little imagination it looked like a cooked corn cob. Its shape was exactly like that. It also had many seeds, like a corn cob.

"Ohhh... a grilled corn cob! It is a corn cob, isn't it?" Elenitsa innocently asked, forgetting at once the whole army of broad beans, which could at any moment rise and attack.

On the spot, Josephine's mind was conjuring up an idea for a hoax. She would feed her friend some of that strange looking plant that looked like corn cob but which she was sure wasn't. If her friend managed to eat this thing, in the end they would both laugh their hearts out. She cut some and holding it by its green spear, she offered it to her. Elenitsa, trying to push aside her half tied hair bow from her eyes, asked again innocently.

"What if your mother scolds us?"

"My mother says to eat so we can grow! Eat it! Or else I'll eat it!" Elenitsa was convinced and after the first good bite, she realized that it was anything but corn cob. It was soooo bitter! She was screaming and the only word that could be made out was "*hoooot!*"

That time too, grandpa had come to her aid first. He immediately understood as soon as he saw the bitten plant thrown on the ground and the little girl foaming from the mouth.

Chapter 3   Grandpa, Mario's father.

"*Dear me, out of all possible things, you found dragon-root to eat?*" and taking her in his arms, he ran towards the garden water tap. Holding her against him with one hand, he continuously gave her water with the other, telling her to spit it out each time. Then, grandpa turned to Lela, who together with Augusta, was running after him without knowing what was going on, and kept asking "*...where are you taking the child grandpa, tell me, where are you taking her?...*" and asked her to bring him some honey to soften the child's mouth and throat. Josephina was stroking Elenitsa's legs, which were hanging from grandpa's lap and apologized.

Even though it was all over, Elenitsa's heart was still beating fast. There were no more tears in her eyes but she continued to breathe in sobs. Augusta approached so she could take her in her arms but the little girl hung from grandpa's neck, clung on to him and kissed both his cheeks, she didn't want to change laps.

"*Do you know what I want of you now?*" grandpa grabbed the opportunity.

"*Never to cast stones at us again! No more stone casting wars! Will you do that?*"

She promised she would, nodding her little head. And she kept her word.

LILY TSONI

IN THE TOWN, there were the Municipal drinking fountains. Municipal, just like the Municipal School, the Municipal Park, Municipal Theatre and Municipal Hospital. Just like that. People waited to fill their jugs with water, forming queues in front of them, according to the zeitgeist of the times since there queues everywhere. Queues for the cinema, queues for the Winter or Summer Stage of the Municipal Theatre; especially whenever there was a shoal of visitors from Athens. There was a queue for the hairdresser's, queue for the grocer's and, people were even forming queues for the baker's and the greengrocer's and the butcher's too.

They were made of iron and were rectangular with their upper end curved. They looked a lot like the milestones which stood upright along the national highway and showed the kilometric distance in red numbers. At the top, they had a big, bronze, round button, just like the one the old alarms clocks had. They would press it and water would flow. The water made its way there from the springs of the mountain range close by, which towered in the northeast of the town and stopped where the ocean disappeared.

LELA WAS only seventeen years old when her mother died. Josephina's grandmother had intervened then -because Lela was suddenly left all alone in the world- to stay with Augusta for a little while until Lela decided what to do next. She hadn't finished school yet. She began in the final year of course, the month after she moved to Augusta's house. After finishing school

Chapter 4   The loose, woolen vermilion dress
             with the lace collar and the blue bow.

she carried on with her English studies, whilst at the same time offering to help Augusta with the housework. She adopted responsibilities and took initiative and felt at home there. In the end, she had decided not to continue with university studies after high school, at least for the time being, or so she said. She missed her family a lot and felt very lucky that she'd found a supportive haven and thus decided to stay with them and grew up with Josephina, feeling as if she were her little sister. Each month they deposited a certain amount in the bank for her for the help she gave, even though then Lela heard about it, she that just the fact that she lived with them, was very important for her and that it was shameful that she was also paid, at the time when she felt as if they were her family.

Lela really liked to go from time to time to the municipal water fountain of the neighborhood just before noon or early in the afternoon, not to gather water, like the rest who stood there in a queue, but to listen to some gossip, the kind that the charwomen told about everything that happened in their Ladies' homes. They, on the other hand, pretended that it was more convenient to get water from the fountain for their laundry and thus save water for the family, when in reality it was an opportunity to let off steam and entertain themselves even though their hands and arms suffered as a result of carrying one bucket of water after another. On that morning, as she had come back from an English lesson, she said she'd go to the fountain for a while, as usually. Before leaving the garden, Josephina had jumped out in front of her from a cluster of bushes pretending to be a cuckoo and *had made out of her skin* as Lela had told her. It was only a short while since she used to leave her in the kiosk to play with her dolls, surrounded by a dozen books from the *"Lilika"* and *"Martine"* series which, because they had read them to her so many times, she knew by heart, inside out and back to front and now she read them out loud to her dolls, whilst looking at the pictures. But that's what Josephine always did. They'd leave her somewhere and she'd show up somewhere else. She spun around Lela two or three times like a top, holding the hem of her dress, almost knocked her over and then decided to stop. She asked Lela to take her with her. Augusta, who was looking at them through a window on the top floor, nodded to her in agreement as soon as Lela lifted her eyes in search of her.

They set out for the fountain hand in hand. The women at the fountain were laughing laudly and whispering and kept throwing stealthy glances at the *"Americana's"* house.

Lela was immediately absorbed by the news of the day. They were talking about old Thanasso who worked at that two-storey house on the corner, which was painted renaissance pink and the doors and windows ochre.

It was George's, the pharmacist's house, the Greek-American with a big flower always in his lapel and, usually a carnation or a gardenia or a rosebud and a cigar in his mouth; all day! He lived there with his American wife and the neighborhood of course called her, not Joan, it sounded too odd to Greek ears, but *Americana* Even when they addressed her or greeted her, most of the neighbors didn't call her by her name.

Chapter 4   The loose, woolen vermilion dress
           with the lace collar and the blue bow.

They called her *Mrs. - Georgena* -which meant *Georgis's wife*- or even *Mrs.-Americana*.

Whenever Lela was in Joan's presence, she took great care to beat her tongue rather than blurt out *"Americana"* and she managed to call her simply *"Mrs. Joan"*. This was the result of Augusta's insistence on making Lela think before she spoke, especially about things which seemed impolite and were far removed from the good manners that Lela was supported to possess. And Lela had good manners and a good upbringing but sometimes she forgot or that 'something' slipped out, that *"a girl should never forget if she wants to be sweet and cute, because all women ought to be sweet and cute"* Augusta always used to say.

SO, AS THE story goes, at the back of Georgis's house, there was a well with artesian water. Georgis, as a good pharmacist, with a lot of additional knowledge in various fields of medicine, worked meticulously with the quality of that water, they said. He had even sent a sample to America, he said, only to conclude that his family would drink the water of that well and no other because it was precious. "You drink and you are nourished" he would always say.

Now Thanasso, who did all the household chores and only went home at nights to sleep, didn't have good teeth. She was always suffering from toothaches in the beginning when they'd first hired her six years earlier. She smelt of ouzo and tsipouro which she glutted herself with so she could ease the pain. As a result, she'd leave a trail of stench in every room of the house tough which she had passed, and it was unbearable for both Joan and Georgis, even though the truth was that there weren't many things that weren't unbearable for him. Everything around him was at fault. Joan had taken her to the dentist and he had taken all her teeth out and had made her a set of dentures. Georgis had given it to her as a present after giving in to pressure from his wife because he had had other plans in mind. He had been thinking of having Thanasso work for them without pay until she squared up with him for the denture. Joan, however, was too much of a Lady to allow and accept something like that from a poor, lonely old woman. So, the story had it, that the previous day, Thanasso was above the well drawing water. *"Like a lady hawk!"* one of the gossipers of the fountain remarked and the rest stifled their uproarious laughter by covering their mouths with their hands – as if they were all keyed for the same movement. Thanasso was turning the windlass of the well and pumping water, when she heard Joan calling *"Tanasso where are you? Tanassoooo!"* and Thanasso or *Tanasso* in the American way, responded with all her might. *"I'm here Mrs. Joaaaan!"* but as soon as she opened her mouth, her false teeth flew out and fell into the well!

"Just like the Lady Hawk!" iterated the same woman.

The rest of the women didn't seem to understand though because the Lady Hawk of the song had fallen into the well together with her bracelets... She couldn't stop crying for the dentures that had fallen and now what teeth would she have? For her employers, who would surely scold her since they had paid a fortune for her false teeth which to add insult to injury had fallen inside the well that meant so much to Georgis. Moreover, Georgis was a very fastidious and ill-mannered man and loathed the air he breathed if another was standing too close to him. Every morning, he'd ask her if she had washed her denture. Then he'd ask if she had washed her

Chapter 4 The loose, woolen vermilion dress with the lace collar and the blue bow.

hands before cooking and after lunch – because she ate at their home – he'd send her to clean her teeth again and Joan would rebuke him because he was so finicky. Georgis saw germs everywhere and would constantly say: *"Look, there are a lot of germs here!"* and poor Thanasso would stoop to finally see these germs, but they could never be seen. Georgis saw them though, yes that's for sure. *"He's educated! That's why he sees such things"* thought Thanasso. *"How could I possibly know about such matters? How could I possibly see 'em?"* She'd bend over again hoping for a miracle so the germs would be revealed.

The rumors had travelled faster than the speed of light and went around not only the neighbourhood but the whole town as well and everyone was talking about Thanasso's false teeth. She was talked about by people who didn't even know her! It was said that supposedly, the Americana had quarreled very badly with Georgis -as she was a commiserative lady even though she was a *foreigner* because he wanted to send Thanasso away. While they had been fighting, he had sent Thanasso to call the blacksmith from the corner forge and had him seal the well because he was now disgusted by the well water owing to the fact that it now had a pair of dentures lying at the bottom of it. It was also said that the Americana loved Thanasso and trusted the poor woman, not to mention that she had the benefit of her for company and learnt Greek from her which made Thanasso feel very self-important.

"Tanasso is like a mommy to me!" Joan kept repeating, because Thanasso was about the same age as Georgis, and the Americana was less than half of his age and that was something that bewildered all of them, even Augusta who was ahead of her time. How could a young, beautiful, intelligent woman with a perfect disposition marry an old geezer like Georgis! He was handsome at first sight until he opened his mouth, he was rather ill-mannered though and more often than not rude, and never ever backed down even if he knew he was at fault, while the word *sorry* was never used. He was also waggish, as he would go jogging every morning with that hair-net on his head which covered all of his head to the eyebrows, so that his hair wouldn't get messy in his sleep or whilst out jogging.

Joan was the daughter of a Franco-Levantine merchant and a Mauritian Creole. She was born in America and raised among nuns. In addition to her own mother tongue, she spoke French, Italian, German, Russian and Latin American. She had studied ballet and was very proficient at playing the piano and the harpsichord. She had met Georgis at a gala after a concert in Boston. A fortuitous event and his love for the piano were maybe the only things that brute had in common with natty Joan. These things ended up in a great love and respect between them but which still seemed odd to everybody else. When Joan had asked him if they could live in Greece, Georgis repatriated.

The Americana's indulgence was never denied and thus they kept Thanasso. The well was sealed up by the blacksmith on the same evening, with a huge metal plate and was locked with four fat padlocks. Joan also got him to promise that they'd give Thanasso some new dentures and on that very same evening, she escorted Thanasso to the dentist.

AND THEY kept on talking about Thanasso and her teeth, her old ones and her new ones and kept laughing. And Lela

Chapter 4   The loose, woolen vermilion dress
            with the lace collar and the blue bow.

was so taken in and paid such close attention so as not to miss a word from Thanasso's pratfall that she ended up loosing Josephina...

The cross-road with the big plane tree and the fountain were about ten meters away from the unguarded railroad track and you could now hear the train whistling in the distance, getting closer.

"Why don't I go check on the child?" Augusta thought. *"Lela is sometimes absentminded and Josephine on the other hand, slips away right under your nose..."* Throwing *"The Monastery of Parma"* on a chair and straightening out her hair, she looked out through the sun lounge, drawing back the curtains.

On the other side of the train tracks, the little girl was already making her way back home. Alone. Without Lela who was nowhere in sight. Augusta's mind went blank. For seconds, she froze. The new train whistle, closer this time, jerked her back to life. She yanked the door open with such power that it banged against the wall and then slammed loudly behind her. She descended the few steps that brought her on to the garden lawn almost leaping over it. She ran down the path which seemed miles in length. Her skirt got caught up on the thorns of an evergreen thistle and was torn. At long last, she was through the garden gate. For the first time, Lela's habit of leaving the gate wide open upon her exit had been useful.

The train continued to whistle.
She could hear it getting closer and closer. Her heels almost reached her ears as she ran. She was running as fast as she could. She started going up the small acclivity towards the tracks.
Josephina was doing the same thing on the other side. The train kept on whistling. The little girl was now in the middle of the rails right between the two tracks. She was smiling to Augusta, waving her hand. There were hardly five or six meters between the train and the girl. Augusta was burning but she felt all her limbs frozen and her heart beating like a tom-tom in the merciless rhythm of the jungle. What she wanted more than anything else was to save her child. And the only thing missing at that moment were her legs. Augusta managed not to faint but her legs wouldn't hold her anymore. She stopped walking. Only a miracle would now save her daughter. Crawling on the sharp, white rocks at the side of the tracks, she stretched out her hands, which she struggled in vain to keep steady, and grabbing the hem of the little girl's dress, she pulled her out of the train tracks, dragging her like a sack over the rails, onto the jagged rocks and then onto her. In the next second, the train was hollering like a demon beside them. It wasn't only the incessant whistling. It was the sound of the steam engine.
It was the iron wheels which rolled over the iron rails producing sparks. It was all this put together.
The engine-driver was hanging half in and half out of the train, driving with terror painted on his face and his eyes shut tight so that he wouldn't see the horror that was about to take place. The breaking of the train was a hard task. It required several miles and plenty of time to come to a halt and he knew this quite well. He had seen the child in front of him at the last minute and he felt helpless to do anything to save it. From

Chapter 4   The loose, woolen vermilion dress
             with the lace collar and the blue bow.

the other side of the tracks, the women stooped so that they could see between the carriages, which were speeding like hell and looked as if they had no space between them, or their wheels, whether the child was safe. They were unable to find out until the last wheels of the last carriage had rolled.

So they stood side by side, terrified and motionless as if in a sophisticated tableau vivant[12]. Lela among them.

Augusta was holding Josephina tightly and did not have the strength to cry... and she wanted to so much... Lela was as white as a ghost. *"And now, they'll rid of me!"* she said to herself, convinced that it would be justified.

"Come, help me get up..." Augusta asked of her. *"It's over now!"* she said and kissed her child's head. She didn't scold Lela right then. She would say what she had to say later when Josephine wasn't present. Lela didn't apologize either. She would also do it later in the day. She would have plenty of time to apologize. Augusta herself was the one who had taught her not to rush. *"Wait for the most right time not just the right time"* she would say to her.

As for the beautiful, loose, woolen vermilion dress with the lace collar and the blue bow that Josephine was wearing that day, it was never to be worn again; which was as the little girl wished.

---

[12] French in text: *"living picture"*; once (before radio, film and television) popular form of entertainment used to recreate painting *"on stage"*. A group of actors who don't speak or move throughout the duration of the display.

55

A UGUSTA AND Mario's house was swamped with greenery.
It was surrounded by ivy, zibeline and ampelopsis. Only the doors and windows were left uncovered. Augusta herself had brought herself, from the forest beside Mario's village, the ivy and the zibeline. Alekos the florist, the only one in town, had brought her the ampelopsis. He helped her with the planting. He planted ivy at the base of the trees and it started to quickly climb their trunks.

On the left and right of the stone path there were stone flower beds with a profusion of flowers and trees. The whole garden was a lilliputian paradise. Roses, tulips and firethorns, Chinese apple trees and dahlias, oleanders, pine trees, brigalows and a plane tree that had been there for years and years before the house was built and where a thick rope with a round seat hewn out wood hung from its thickest branch so Josephina could swing. Sour cherry trees and cherry trees, fir trees, orange trees and two almond trees which each produced white and pink flowers respectively.

The fence of the stone barton and its wall were embosomed by passion flowers and wisterias. At the end of the garden there was a gazebo. It was an octagonal wooden structure with the wood interwoven all around in a thick beautiful lattice which formed an octagonal cupola with an iron weathercock on top. Augusta had designed the rooster on the weather- vane and the blacksmith, who had his smithy shop near their house, had made it. Mario had brought in

Chapter 5   Flowers' "Coiffures".

craftsmen from Epirus, from Giannena[13], to build his house. The same men made that stone path in the garden which looked like cobblestone paving. They covered the rest of the yard in the same way wherever there wasn't a flower bed and short grass grew between the stones.

On the south side of the garden, where it bordered Mrs. Veneco's garden, there were four olive trees planted on a row. Next to the last one there was a wooden electricity pylon. On its top, storks had been building their nests for years before the house was built.
They were impressive and Josephina asked eagerly all the time *"when are the storks coming"*. She waited for them to come each year. She'd stand under the pylon and would sing the same song to them that her grandmother, and also Augusta, sang to them, when they were little.
"White stork, go to your nest, the snake is near, it'll eat your eggs..." She'd also sing an Italian song which she had been taught by Mario, who was in turn taught by Antonio back in the days of the occupation of the country.
"Lo sai che I papaveri son' alti, alti, alti, ma tu sei piccolina, sei nata paperina, che cosa ci puoi far'..."[14]
Together with the storks, came the swallows. They had built their nests under the tiles of the house and nested there despite the objections from Lela who -when it was her turn- was obliged to clean up their mess daily. But *"Swallows are bliss!"* Augusta used to say.

---

[13] Stone craftsmen from the area in and around the town of *Giannena (Ioannina)*, in the North West part of Greece, were very famous.

[14] Italian in the text: *"You know the poppies are tall, tall, tall, but you are small, you are born like the duckling (meaning you are short) and what can you do about that?"*

On the first day of March, Augusta would always place a bracelet on her daughter's hand which was made of three strings, white, red and golden, twisted tightly around each other which made them look like one. It was called a "*march*" and it was worn as protection from the March sun.

"He who has a precious daughter, let not the sun of March, lay his eyes upon her" they said. Josephina wore the *march* until Easter. Then, on Easter day, she'd take it off and tie it on the Easter Lamb's leg. After the spitting, they'd again take it off and Josephina would take it and leave it on a tree in the garden, on a branch that she could reach or on some flower. From there, either the swallows or the storks would take it and adorned their nest with it...
And March would pass, and April would come. April would also pass on by and May would arrive. The little lady of the house spent many hours in the garden.

IT WAS THEN that she played her game. A game played by her own rules. Without cheating and without being annoyed by other children's cheating. She'd play the game all by herself. And she avoided telling or teaching it to anyone else. No matter how much Lela insisted on asking, she never got an answer. She never learnt what she wanted.

"I'd really like to know why you are plucking the flowers! What have they done to you, the poor things? Tell me!" and she went on obviously crossed... *"and the scissors? Where did you find the scissors again? Did you take them from the sewing basket? Haven't we said that scissors and knives aren't allowed? You'll butcher yourself! You can poke your eyes out with them! Haven't we been through that? You can*

Chapter 5   Flowers' "Coiffures".

fall, and with those things in your hand you may injure yourself! Give them here! God help you if you take them again!"

However hard Lela tried to decipher the little girl's game, she couldn't. Josephina stubbornly kept her mouth shut. She'd hand over the scissors, grouching and accusing Lela of always spoiling her game. She, in turn, of course, fumed.

"What game have I spoiled? I don't see any game! Show it to me then, so I can see it and I'll never spoil it for you again! A game, she says!"

A game she played alone and one she alone knew. She and herself... and the flowers of the garden... She had named it *"coiffure of flowers"* in which she pretended to be a hairdresser for the flowers. Her career as a hairdresser hadn't started though with the flowers as her customers...

ONE DAY, she had asked her mother what the sign outside the hairdresser's said. She was referring to Anna's shop where Augusta had her hair done.

"Women's Coiffure, which means hairdos for women and not only hairdos but also haircuts and washing of the hair and all the hair care that a hairdresser does for you" she had explained.

She decided there and then to be a hairdresser. But where? On whose head? She had to find customers! She chose a couple of her dolls. They were to become her first customers. She cut off one of the two braids of the red-haired doll. She had a difficult time. It was the first time she had held a pair of scissors in her hands. Moreover that doll's hair was hard.

Everything on that doll was different. Joan, the pharmacists' wife, had brought it over from America and given it to her. She was half way through the doll with the brown pigtails haircut when the grownups got wind of her and stopped her. Augusta explained that neither does their hair grow because dolls have fake hair nor are scissors good when little children hold them. They become dangerous in little hands and they can hurt them.

She burst into tears. She was holding the braid she had cut off and she was crying. What if mom was right, what would the doll now do without her braid? It never crossed her mind that dolls hair doesn't grow because it's fake and fake hair doesn't grow!

"Well, I'm never going to cut their hair again!" she promised to herself.

A few days later, she looked at herself in the mirror. She would cut her own hair. Her hair wasn't fake and so it would grow back again.
With a crooked haircut and a huge smile she went into the kitchen. Lela was rolling out pastry for the pie with the rolling pin and Augusta was smoothing it out and filling the pie. Some freshly baked, candied red apples, pears and quinces were on the table but the little girl didn't even look at them. Her smile had reached her ears. She had given herself a haircut! She had managed! Her forelocks had been cut into a pitiful zig-zag. At some points they were cut to the roots. Her left eyebrow had also been cut at one spot and it looked like an old scar.
How the rolling pin got into Augusta's hands and from there landed on Josephina's behind, no one could guess! Not even

Chapter 5   Flowers' "Coiffures".

Augusta. She didn't hit her hard. She did it more as a warning so the child would finally understand that what she was doing was very wrong. She could have blinded herself with those scissors.

Today she had used the big sewing scissors and was still holding them in her hands. She had descended all those stairs from her bedroom to the kitchen. She could have tripped and fallen on those stairs and could have hurt herself. She scolded her secondly. These doings of hers were very dangerous. She had to finally stop pretending to be a hairdresser even by means of threats. The little one though wouldn't give up that easy. Between her sobs she found the courage to announce the happy medium that had just formed inside her little

mind. She was going to exercise the practice of hairdressing despite the grownups hounding her!

"Then, let me cut Lela's hair with the small scissors!"

Lela took a fright *"Good Lord! You'll feign to be a hairdresser, girl, you can find someone else to be your guinea pig, as my mother said? Not on me! Mrs. Augusta, do something!"*

In the end, Josephina didn't seem to be convinced that she should never ever h again hold either the big scissors or the small ones in her hands. Never again should she hold another pair of scissors, big or small. She was convinced, however, that she should never cut anyone's hair again, ever.
Neither her dolls' nor her own or her friends' hair. She still wanted to be a hairdresser though but she didn't have any customers and she had to find some. She racked her brains for an idea and in the end, she came up with one!

MINA, THE tall, svelte neighbor with the black hair which she dyed raven black and combed in an impressive yet rather odd manner, passed by in the street. She was, as always, heavily made-up with black eyeliner on the eyes and brows, with pretty blusher and red lipstick. She was also crammed inside her really tight dress with the big scoops in the neck and back, the thick belt around her waist and the tiny slit in the back of the skirt. She had perfect proportions and showed them off daily, wearing close-fitting, really chic and skin-tight clothes. She even wore her coats, cloaks and jackets skin-tight. They suited her though, very much because beyond having the perfect proportions she also had a beautiful posture. Her clothes were of the same color as her hair. Black. No one ever recalled *Dahlia* wearing any other color of clothing except black.

"*Dahlia is passing by!*" Lela had told Augusta and she scolded her because if Mina had heard her calling her *Dahlia* she might resent it. Of course, Mina was aware of her nickname. Several years before, some of those students that come and go to school on foot from the neighboring villages, were the ones that gave it to her. It wasn't however, the most courteous thing for her to hear Lela calling her by her nick name.
They had named her *Dahlia* because with a little imagination, Mrs. Mina's short hair, which she held up with a bunch of hairpins, drowned in brilliantine and emptied a whole can of hairspray on every day and then fashioned it all upwards, reminded the children of Dahlia.
That's exactly how her hair was upturned: in pointy upward elf-locks identical to a fully blossomed dahlia, starting from the highest part of the nape of the neck to the top of her head.

Chapter 5   Flowers' "Coiffures".

The front part of her hair had the same upward direction but was gathered at the top part of her forehead, like a light, conscientious *featherless raven.*

Since there was a woman who answered to the name *Dahlia*, why shouldn't there be flowers which feign to be Ladies.

She was going to give haircuts to the flowers of the garden! The flowers from now on would be her customers. The whole garden would now be her own, her very own Beauty Salon. She'd play her own secret game with them.

SHE named it without much hesitation *"Coiffure of flowers"* and when she grew up she may become a real hairdresser and cut real hair and have real customers. Until then though, she'd comb and give haircuts to the flowers. She didn't give her secret away to anyone. It would be her very own secret. She wouldn't share it with anyone!

"And you? How would you like your hair? A bun, a banana bun? Very good! But, you do need a little trim, though!" The little pair of scissors that she had secretly taken from her mother's vanity case would cut in an instant the hair of the blonde lady who was no other than a yellow daisy.

All the yellow flowers in the garden were her blonde customers. The white and ivory ones were the old ladies with their white hair. The rest of the colors, from pink to red, blue and bordeaux were the red heads and the brunettes and the black haired women.

She'd imagine that each Dahlia-customer was Mrs. Mina's twin sister.

She'd roll the big leaves of the flowers like *dolmadakia* (stuffed vine leaves with rice). Then, she'd wrap the petals around a pencil and fix them in place with a clothes peg in order to form them. Then she'd place them under the hair dryer, which was a small, tin kettle borrowed from the kitchen utensils she had for her dolls.

Mrs. Rose had split ends and the little hairdresser would clear her stem of her tiny thorns, with the tip of the scissors. She'd perm their hair by mixing up their petals so they'd look curly like the curls of a perm. The most painless hairdressing tool in her hands was the hair-net. The role of the hair-net was played by a small piece of an old rope net for shopping which she found in a drawer. And the flower petals kept falling, clipped to the ground.

And Lela kept asking never getting an answer. Josephine kept her mouth well shut. However well they hid away the scissors of the house, she always found a way to hunt them out.

And sometimes the grownups were at fault even though they scolded her, for there were plenty of times that they'd accidentally leave the scissors outside their hiding place...

Chapter 6   A bouquet for Her Majesty the Queen.

THAT SPRING, King Paul and Queen Frederique were going to tour the cities of the country. Georgis, the pharmacist, was a royalist. Joan the Americana, his wife, took delight in all the social events where the people shouted *Hurray* and wore their best clothes. She had grown up with celebrations in America and in Greece there was always some kind of anniversary to celebrate. And if there wasn't, she'd create one. And she always succeeded and everybody acknowledged that. Whenever she informed Georgis that some anniversary or another was approaching and they "had to celebrate it", even Georgis, who would whine for days on end because he was antisocial, he was mean with money, and celebrations needed money, seemed content by the end of the night; even if he wished before the night started *"I hope no one arrives"* and as the night continued *"I hope they all get the hell out of here"* so he could have his peace and quiet.

On that occasion she had persuaded him quite easily. Joan was going to offer the Queen a bouquet. She wanted Georgis' approval, although not for the bouquet but for the new outfit that she would have to wear on such a day. Of course Georgis, even coercively, always did her favors, whatever they were; even the expensive ones, despite the fact that his heart ached! On this particular occasion, in order for him to be fairly content so that Joan wouldn't be faced with some ban at the last minute -where they would both look foolish- Georgis had reported his wife's desire publically to the police, the Mayor and the local authorities in writing as well.
Following this, the Master of Ceremonies included in the ceremonial programme
 "...offering of a bouquet to Her Majesty The Queen from the honorable resident of our town, etc..."

Joan, of course, from the minute she set her mind on offering a bouquet to the crowned Lady who was to visit their town, counted on Augusta's roses.

"Will you give me some roses, Augusta? I would like them for the queen! Well, how about thirty white roses? Do you agree, yes?" she had asked Augusta in her broken Greek.

Augusta promised. Even if Joan had asked for twice as many, she would have given them to her. She had five or six rose bushes and the one with the white roses, was huge. It took up a whole flower bed all by itself.

One day before the crowned guests arrived, Joan went over to Augusta's to see the roses. They were wonderful. There were some rosebuds, some flowers in full bloom and others half open. She would make her bouquet using the rosebuds and the half open ones. She was going to wrap them in snow-white lacework that Thanasso was crocheting especially for the occasion; this was going to be given as a gift to the queen together with the bouquet.

ON THE DAY of the royal visit, Joan went to fetch the roses at the crack of dawn. She couldn't sit still. She wanted to prepare the bouquet so she would have time left for her own preparations. According to the programme, the guests with their escorts would arrive at eleven. Lela was yawning and searching for the key to the gate. Not even Mario had left yet. As soon as Lela opened the door, she ran straight towards the big white rose bush.

"Has she been dreaming about those flowers all night? The day has hardly dawned yet!" she muttered to herself feeling annoyed to have her sleep disturbed. Joan had already spoilt the silence of the morning and that of the garden, which even the birds respected.

Chapter 6   A bouquet for Her Majesty the Queen.

"That's why they call them crazy-americanas" Lela muttered under her breath again...

"Catastrophe! It's a great catastrophe! The greatest one of all!"

Some sparrows which were nestling in the flowerbeds flew away in fear. So did the pigeons from the Mrs. Veneko's roof tiles. Two storks flew away snapping their beaks and flapping their wings loundly. Augusta dashed outside without slippers having got a scare with all that *catastrophe* Joan was shouting about in English so early in the morning. *"At noon yesterday, they were here! And here! And.... here they were! Oh my God! Oh mon Dieu! Oh mon Dieu!"* She cried and protested and turned from one flower bed to another, clutching her hands in despair.

Augusta sympathized with her immediately! Joan was right to shout blue murd! Some of the roses from the white rose bush were still in place, but some were cut, some mixed up due to... the perms, and others were lying on the ground of the flowerbed or the flagstone paving. Josephine had got hold of all of them! Joan kept on pleading with God, partly in English and partly in French. Her tongue couldn't cope with pleading in Greek. She touched the cut rosebuds with her palms whenever they weren't touching her cheeks which had turned pale. Augusta didn't know what to say although she knew who had done it. The huge white rose bush, which had been full of rosebuds and half open roses twenty-four hours ago, now looked bombarded! All the white roses looked pathetic and pitiful.

"Joan, don't you worry! We'll find other flowers! The garden has a whole bunch of flowers! We'll find something! Please!

Calm down!" Augusta tried in vain to calm her American friend. *"It's not the end of the world!"*

"Ochi! Ochi![15] *No, no, no! Ochi! Only these were ideal! Oh mon Dieu!*[16] *But why are they like that? Is it the snails? Yes? Is that it? The snails"* Joan asked full of anguish. *"De escargots*[17]*? Is it de escargots? Is that it?"*

"I know exactly which snail is to blame, Joan, and I'll take care of it later! Right now, it's sleeping! Come on, now, let's see what we can do about it! We have to find something... Alekos the florist won't have white roses either.... He never stocks white! I have got some pretty muguet,[18] *Joan. Wouldn't you like a bouquet of muguet? We'll place some of their leaves all around them and they'll be even prettier than the roses! Come!"*

In a corner of the garden, Augusta kept muguet. It was her favourite flower. Joan's grey-blue eyes lit up! The muguet were wonderful!

"Oh, Lilies of the Valley! Ces, sont mes fleurs favourits! Augusta! Augusta ! Thank you!" She went on with her *mon Dieus* and her *my Gods* but this time out of pleasure. She started asking Augusta again what she meant by saying that she knew '*which snail'* had done it.

*"Is it perhaps Mario? He did it? He doesn't love the Queen

---

[15] Greek in text: "*No! No!*"

[16] French in text: "*Oh, my God!*"

[17] French in text: "*The snails? Is it the snails?*"

[18] French in text: *Le muguet* (or *Le Muguet de mai*), is the *Lily of the Valley*.

Chapter 6   A bouquet for Her Majesty the Queen.

and he cut the white roses? Yes? This Mario is the escargots of the garden?"

"You've got a vivid imagination Joan! If Mario hears you, he will get mad! He may not particularly like royal families much, I don't really know.... but he would never do this! You hear me? Never! It's my daughter who did it! She likes cutting the flowers! I don't know why, but she likes it. She must have cut them yesterday evening, I guess", she explained and went on to cut the muguet.

"The Lilies of the Valley" made a wonderful bouquet. It was presented by Joan dressed in her white, rendingote style manteau. She also wore, short white gloves, something which was mandatory due to the formality of the day and which was allowed because of her trois-quart sleeves. She also wore a tiny hat of the same material as her cloak, similar to the one that the Pope wears. She was beautiful.

Queen Frederique was impressed. Joan gave her the bouquet, taking a small graceful curtsey. Joan seemed to know about these things. She looked really happy that everything had gone well and she not only saw this in the eyes and admiration of the noble lady but also in the admiring of her fellow citizens.

Later everyone spent much time talking about the noble guests, but also about the elegance of manners of Joan the American as well as her beautiful bouquet.

"SHALL WE throw a party?" And they'd throw one. And then... *blame it on the bossa-nova*... It wasn't necessary for these parties to be arranged before hand. Most people decided to throw one at the last minute and all of them turned out to be very successful. Parties and live music. Under the arbor and the moon, when there was one. Under the light bulbs of the garden, when there wasn't. Every neighborhood had its own orchestra.

Teddy boys with *quiffs, pompadours* and *crew* cuts. In their high-waist pipe trousers or five-pocket jeans and leather jackets. In colored socks, *Beatle* boots and winkle pickers. And the one, who had the best voice in the orchestra, would also sing; a wonderful Greek, British, American, French and Italian hit parade.

Bodies cramped inside elegant, figure-hugging and skin tight dresses. Huge erect collars for the fanatics of the blotter and whalebone for those who had a waist like a ring and skirts,

Chapter 7   Good for the Americana.

fluffy like umbrellas. There really were a lot of skirts... *bubble* skirts and *twirling poodle* skirts but *pencil* skirts as well, with beautiful details in stripes, polka-dots and floral.

Nicely defined busts. Necks, that protruded all around, and beautifully naked, through deep, loose, triangle and oval neck lines. Slits, which continued all the way down the back and finished as low as they could.
Stockings with seams and *stiletto* heels. Iron heels. Pointy toes. The feet would catch fire from all that dancing in the pointy shoes and the iron heels. The *stiletto* heels would then be cast aside and the ladies would dance barefoot.

At the end of the night, with the help of her escort, she would search for her lost pumps like a genuine Cinderella of her time. Of course, elegance was not necessarily cramped inside the beautiful tight-fitting sheath floral dresses. So, there were also nice drop-waists, cocktail dresses, halter-necked dresses, and narrow shouldered trapeze dresses that flared gently at the bottom. Cute, loose, *A-line* dresses as well as *tent* dresses. Charm College skirts in soft flannel. Overalls and divided skirts, jacquard and mohair pullovers, *v-neck* shirts, elastic slacks with elastic bands under the soles -a fashion stolen from jodhpurs- and tight slacks which left the ankles uncovered and had a small slit at the side of the calf, a fashion borrowed from the fishermen of Capri.

Hula hoop shoes; *Mary Jane* shoes; flat *Russia* leather shoes with huge bows. Broad baby and crepe-soled shoes and low-heeled boots. Thick pantyhose, in black, grey, red and brown. When the hair wasn't pin straight and long, when it wasn't done up in a *banana bun* and when it wasn't the perfect frame cut or a *Charleston* or *á la garçon*[19], it was a *pixie cut* or a *pony tail* or whatever, provided that it was accompanied by the obligatory, wide, elastic hair band. Always in black for the blondes and always in white or pretty polka-dots for the brunettes and the darker ones.

The brilliantine fell lavishly in the palms of the escorts, freezing the shortest hairs on the hardest *quiff*.
Sideburns, which were meticulously trimmed as if a ruler had been used.
Close shaves. Moustaches, when there were any, were so well-tended that they looked as if they were drawn on their faces. Nice handkerchiefs, in the chest pockets. Ties, narrow and necessary. Fine brogue shoes, often in black and white. Moccasin shoes. The toes of the shoes, narrow. Piped pants with cuffs.
Vests and shoulder straps, accessories for few and for all. The overall general appearance, right as a trivet. And every escort who respected himself had to know all the steps of every dance so he could lead his partner.

ONE OF THE annual parties, thrown by Joan the Americana, was for hers and Giorgi's wedding anniversary. It always took place in summer. The other one was thrown for her birthday, in winter, on New Year's Eve.

Joan's birthday party; the biggest social event of the town! It was the Christmas spirit; it was also the fairytale-like

---

[19] French in text: *Boyish (*meaning hair cut *"boyishly"*).

Chapter 7   Good for the Americana.

decorations of Joan's house which differed from the rest; it was how the hostess managed her ideas, time and money; it was all in all Joan's taste which was meticulous and the result always brought about a festive warmth. It was all of the above.

The seamstresses always awaited Joan's party as if they were anticipating a wedding. There were plenty of guests who'd sew a gown for each of Joan's parties. These seamstresses were creative and very expensive; at least the good ones, those with the good name. That's why their customers paid a fortune, knowing that those seamstresses with their handy girls didn't spit blood on the details and on night shifts for nothing, ensuring well-sewn clothes for the significant event, which resembled an informal fashion show for different budgets, styles and tastes which went on all night long. Bodices full of spangles and beads, tiffanies and velvets, crepe satins and silks, taffetas and organdies. Combinations that were lustrous, eruptive and gentle, daring and conservative.

The guests looked like Hollywood divas and gen premier dandies. The hostess shone. The host whined silently, in his own sullen way, as always. At the end of the night however, he always congratulated his wife and claimed to be happy... only because their guests had finally got the hell out of his way...

THAT YEAR for the first time, Joan didn't wear one of her gowns which she always brought from America because they resembled romantic ballet tutus. Given that she was a lover of romantic ballet mainly and the *Marie Taglioni*[20] three-quarter, tutu skirts, Joan made a difference this time, putting

---

[20] Italian-Swedish famous ballerina (*Romantic* ballet).

aside her balletomania as well as all her *pointe* ballerina pumps: from those she had kept ever since she was a little girl and they were tiny to her latest ones which she had danced *La Sylphide*[21] in, hanging as always in their conspicuous place inside their living room. And she left Georgis wondering, not so much as to why his wife had abandoned the *"Marie Taglioni ballet style"* -he didn't even know if there was such

a style- but more as to how Joan would welcome her guests, as a hostess, *in that thing*. And *that thing* was no other than the cute mini skirt by Mary Quant, the British fashion designer[22], which was also handmade. Joan had bought it on her last return from New York when she stopped for *a couple of days* in London, as she tended to say, even if she stayed there for a week. She had kept it in her wardrobe for days now; she'd take it out, try it on making sure no one saw her in it and anxiously anticipated wearing it on her birthday. Once more, she had put a full stop to Georgis's objections, handling Georgis in the way only she knew how and which she hadn't

---

[21] Ballet created by Marie Taglioni's choreographer father exclusively for her (1832); known as the first ballet where dancing *en pointe (on toes)* for first time had *an aesthetic rationale*. Also known as Marie *shortened her ballet skirt* in the performance of *La Sylphide* (scandal!); her father wanted everyone to see how excellent his daughter was dancing *en pointe*.

[22] The famous and popular daughter of the Welsh schoolteachers, who at the right time ('60s), in the right place (swinging London), used her own unique talent and created the *Mary Quant* new wave movement of fun and fantasy in fashion making her clothes part of the *London look* and her name synonymous with trendiness.

Chapter 7   Good for the Americana.

invented solely for her fractious husband; it was simply the way she spoke, confident and cute without leaving room for the slightest hint of a doubt... and Georgis always raised his hands in frustration.

"Finally my Georgis, the women can now run to get the bus and get on it quickly with this skirt... as they say in London... And this Mary Quant with her mini, is a... the... how do you say... a... yes... a real thing! This is how the women will dress from now onwards! And... am I not your pretty wife anymore, inside this pretty mini skirt of mine?" and she twisted herself around, lifting the skirt a little higher on one side, revealing her long pretty calves, beautiful and free, to Georgis and her three-sided mirror. Then, she wore her sleeveless top with the geometrically square neckline and the pattern with the *daisy, margarita-emblem* direct from the London fashion designer, where the heart is. She wore her pretty, wide, white calf boots and Georgis, finally, smiled. He asked her to close her eyes and *stretch* out her hand. He put a thick, wide antique bracelet on her wrist, made of gold and silver. It was his gift for her birthday.

"YOU MIX the white of an egg, with half a bar of green soap flakes and half a glass of ouzo, throw in a piece of Chios mastic if you have any; if you don't, it doesn't really matter. Stir until it becomes a rich cream. A mush that is firm and not watery and falls when you hold it up with a fork... Got it? Spread the mixture on the ribs and wrap a jaconet with a thin weave around them. No other cloth will do because the cream will constrict the cloth and that in turn will constrict the ribs and the patient won't be able to breathe. Go now and when I get myself ready, I'll join you..."

Despite Georgis's sleepless night due to the New Year's Eve party, he was already wide awake, offering a practical solution to Lela's problem. A solution, beyond science or as a matter of fact pre-dating it. Georgis, however, was no charlatan. In addition to the medicine of the factories that he sold in his pharmacy; he simply gave out ointments and syrups of his own inspiration.
And those who believed in Georgis's concoctions were plenty. He would hand over the prescription and the drug would be made by his assistant, inside his *"laboratory-laboratoire*[23]*"* as the sign etched in calligraphy.

Lela was now carefully listening to him, hanging on his every word, looking at his mouth when she wasn't looking him straight in the eyes, so as not to miss anything. She repeated after him because he had asked her to.

THE PRESCRIPTION he had given her was for Amalia, Loula's sister. The two little sisters lived an agonizing childhood right under their father's nose! He didn't have a clue as what went on. And when he did find his little girls beaten, disheveled, bruised or scratched and bleeding, choking on their tears, he merely turned a blind eye. Ever since Tasoula had taken their mother's place, the fairytale with the evil stepmother and the virtuous father, manifested itself   the household on a daily basis.

The woman would kick and turn over the kneading trough if the dough, which the little girls had kneaded, was slow to rise. She would make them re-knead the bread, cussing at them.

---

[23] French in text: *laboratory*.

Chapter 7   Good for the Americana.

She would beat them mercilessly with the broomstick if she found even one hair on the floor.

She'd make luckless Loula, the youngest, kneel under the icons and then she would pierce her palms and fingers with a needle. This was her punishment each time the little girl revealed to her father all the torture she put them through. And he simply believed his second wife, as she always managed to persuade him that his children were two little liars who slandered her.

The neighbors were too afraid to intervene, as when they had once tried, they had made the already bad situation, worse... she had kept the two little girls home, forbidding them to go to school for days and starved them on top of everything else.

She had caught little Loula, trying to cut a slice of bread and she beat her up badly, throwing the whole loaf out the window, scaring the passers-by. On that occasion, the loaf had nearly hit the parish priest, who happened to go by at that moment, on the head!

Now, after the New Year's beating, Tasoula, the stepmother, had left, slamming the door behind her. Amalia had tried to crawl out, without making it. The neighbors found her when they managed to open the door after that evil woman had vanished around the corner. Amalia could hardly breathe. Loula had been locked in the dining room.

Mrs. Maria, *la laitiére*[24] -as mademoiselle Marie used to call her and as eventually almost all in the town did too even if they didn't know the meaning of the word- who lived on the

---

[24] French in text: *The milk-woman.*

opposite side of the road, got there first. She started screaming as soon as she saw the little girl lying on the floor. The whole neighborhood gathered around quickly. Cowardly at first, in fear of Tasoula's return, which happened rarely though, because after each beating she'd leave the house and wouldn't return until many hours later.

At that moment, Lela, who had gone to church with Augusta, Mario, grandfather and Josephine for the New Year Day service as soon as the first chime sounded in the night, way before the day broke, returned alone. Mario was very sociable and liked to discuss with lots of people, and Lela had become bored. And so, it happened by chance that she was there from the very beginning. And when the neighbors leaned over the wounded girl, she ran home to get Georgis, as on such a day and hour it would be hard to find a doctor.

Breathless from running, she reached the house and started to ring the bell on the door into the yard. Thanasso scolded Georgis's wolf dogs who were howling and they stopped. She led Lela to the attic, scented with perfumes. It was a bit like an actor's dressing room, with lots of bulbs around the mirrors, wardrobes all around the wall and clothes hung on wooden trolley-wardrobes.

She found him covered in shaving cream. He had one of his cheeks bulging; he was standing with his face very close to his big three sided mirror, he had his legs apart and was shaving slowly and carefully, wearing the bottom part of his red checkered pyjamas and a white mesh t-shirt. A huge white towel, wrapped around his neck and tied back at the nape, covered his chest like an enormous bib. For a second Lela halted in fear of scaring Georgis, causing him to butcher

Chapter 7 Good for the Americana.

himself with that giant yatagan-like razor blade he was holding. Only the barber had a similar one in his barber shop. Luckily, none of this happened. Georgis had seen her through the mirror and had stopped shaving. On another white towel, he carefully wiped the blade. Then, he dragged it two or three times up and down the strop he had hanging from the wall. He placed it on the table and asked her perfunctorily what she wanted so early in the morning.

She told him about little Amalia and how she was beaten. That her ribs hurt and she had difficulty in breathing and added that they must hurry because the little girl was semi conscious. Without a second thought, he recommended the prescription for the "*yiaki*".

"*You make it, together with the others and I'll be there shortly with medicine for the pain*" he told her.

He got there twenty minutes later and gave the little girl two different syrups for the pain. He had a hard time trying to find her pulse on her thin little hand. Fortunately, she wasn't running a temperature. That's when Joan arrived. She looked as if she had just woken up. She had been informed of everything and stated that it was the first time in her life that she had heard of such misery. Grief spread all over her face.

"Oh mon Dieu! Oh mon Dieu![25] I will take the child home with us Georgis! No problem! And the other one! There is another child here! Not a word, Giorgis! Am I understood?" She raised the tone of her voice angrily as he was about to react.

---

[25] French in text: "*Oh my God!*"

Then she asked what it was that they had spread on the child. They explained and when they told her that Georgis had suggested it, she started quibbling with her husband partly in English and at partly in French. She was polite though, even though it was obvious that she didn't agree that he had preferred his informal quack remedies instead of giving her some ointment. While she talked, she was kneeling on the floor beside the couch where the little girl was lying. She was caressing her head but she didn't utter a sound.

"Well, that's final, J' ai compris?"[26] Joan said and stood up. Georgis stated for the last time his one and only objection that the father of the children had to give his consent before they could take them.

"*It would be like stealing otherwise, Joan*" he told her.

"*If he loves his children, I don't really understand how he lets his wife treat them so badly! His o w n children! So, now... the children... both of them, to our home!* " She said and asked him to help her transfer Amalia to her car.

Loula was hitting the door of the dining room with all her might. Tasoula had hung the key on a small nail on the top part of the door so the little girls wouldn't be able to reach it. At some point, they heard her. She explained where they would find the key. They opened the door. She got out. Her eyes were swollen from crying. She had red and blue marks on her arms. Judging by the looks of her braids, everyone understood that Tasoula had pulled and dragged the little girl by the hair. Georgis took her by the hand and she asked,

---

[26] French in text: *"Have you understood?"*

Chapter 7   Good for the Americana.

"Where is Tasoula?" and *"What has she done to Amalia?"* Georgis comforted her. He took out a handkerchief from his pocket and gave it to Loula and she blew her nose and got inside the car with him. No one could believe their eyes when they saw Georgis suddenly being so attentive and kind showing such an elegance of manners, which everyone knew he only showed to Joan. To nobody else. Ever!

"Good for the Americana!"

"See the Americana? She is just like us! Even better!"

"Taking in two children, she has never even seen before is a big thing! Bravo for her! And Georgis? He didn't make a sound! He never spoils any of her indulgences!"

The car with the two little girls set off. On that New Year's Day, Santa Claus, who hadn't come in years, not only came but also gave them the most precious gift…

Whoever happened to be there didn't disperse immediately but rather hung around talking about Joan the Americana with the *golden heart* and the *great fortune* that had come upon the two little orphans from that day on. Georgis informed the District Attorney and the police. The neighbors testified and soon Joan and Georgis adopted them, taking formal responsibility for their upbringing. Amalia and Loula never set foot in their family home again. They had found more love at Joan's side than they could have ever imagined existed. They called her *mom* right from the start and Joan took such delight in it. Georgis, was *dad Georgis* and he flaunted it. Joan saw to financially ensuring their daughters right from the start, lest Georgis changed his mind later. And the two little sisters lived happily ever after…

AT THE photography shop, in the loft as well as in the basement, wherever the photographer had set up his equipment, the photographs kept on coming.
The truth is that the photographer had the first and last say in the posture of the head, the body, the smile, the shadows and the penumbras and the brightness. But these occasions were special, unique and -sometimes- quaint.
It was where he took pictures of brides after their wedding ceremony.

It was where prospective gentlemen of the beauty pageants showed off their muscles, wearing only their athletic underwear or their swim wear. They showed off their beauty and the photographer recommended glistening cream so that even the invisible muscles could show better. It also demanded patience. The prospective gentleman had to pump and deflate his chest like a goose and his arms, his abdomen and thighs in the way the artist asked him to.

Just as a doctor would say *breathe in, hold your breath* or *breathe out*.
It was what the fresh lasses pinned their faith on, where they dared to take the big step for the even more daring deed of their life. An acquaintance, via letter, with an emigrant groom that common matchmakers recommended.

The photograph had to be good. The best. It would travel to America, Canada and even Australia for the candidate groom to see. It was usually a Greek-American, Greek-Canadian or Greek-Australian. He was usually self-made and wealthy; someone who left for the land of the cowboys to get rich, mainly by washing dishes. Or for the land of the kangaroos

Chapter 8   Look at the birdie.

to do something similar. Someone who had made it. Or someone, whose grandparents or parents had succeeded long before he came along, either close or distant relatives.

Sometimes, it happened to be a dasher. A stout. There were of course times when the groom was a good looking and well-kept man of their own age, or at other times older even than the bride's father. Even of the same age as her grandfather! That didn't matter though. Not at all, to be exact, because several girlish dreams could be squeezed inside the suitcase with the dowry.
Those that wanted the groom young, handsome and wealthy.

"*Fairytales*" the matchmakers would say, since one and only one thing was sufficient. This was that the groom was to be on the scale of rich to fabulously rich. With the large demand there was for brides from the home country as... "*better the devil you know...*" which good girl would look at the details of youth and beauty? A rich groom was enough and more than enough.

"*Is it more preferable for the girl to become a spinster?*" the matchmakers would say over and over again. Then there was one more thing.

Every one said that women *break*, *crack* and get old faster than men.

"*The young ones are good, I'm not suggesting otherwise, but the old are safer.*" The matchmakers advised. And they knew.

Quite often there were candidate brides who would wrap themselves up in skin tight foundation garments, which reminded one of a cross between swathed mummies and swaddled babies, and managed to look two to three sizes smaller for the full-length portrait...

So, more often than not, they'd base their chances on a successful shooting. They'd shoot many poses and then they'd choose the best. There was a big demand for the one with the slight slant of the head to the right or the left. With their best smile which the girls kept for as long as the photographer asked them to. Because, he had a big say in this. The girl knew it, he knew it and took advantage of it the best he could.

"Come, I'll shoot a pose like the one I shot the other day for Thymia and the American who saw her went crazy and now Thymia is getting her papers ready for America! I shot the same one for Anthoula and she's also married and expecting a child! She also drove her American mad! This pose is infallible! But I need you to help me! You need to do as I say! Don't move unless if I tell you to! Let's go!"

MEROPI *the old maid* -as they called her when they didn't call her *Meropi the spinster,* neither case out of spite, but to distinguish her from Meropi the teacher- wanted to find a husband. She was well over the age of consent and some called her *granny*. She was a cultivated person, however, with a fairly broad mind for her generation, so she simply answered in a bittersweet way *"Do I have grandchildren without my knowing?"* and she never got angry. At least she never got angry with the others. She got angry with herself however, because she couldn't get angry with her parents who had passed many years ago. Because it was those two departed souls that were to blame, as she claimed, and now she was aging alone. Not that she was having a bad time! Quite the contrary!

Chapter 8   Look at the birdie.

Of course, it is true that Meropi had a wide circle of friends and acquaintances, everyone loved her and, respected her; everyone asked for her opinion and she held a place in everyone's heart.
She was a pleasant person to be with which was why they wanted her. It never crossed anyone's mind to take advantage of her or her fortune -let's call it an inheritance! in the long run. No! No one, ever! And Meropi knew this and was happy about it. She did however yearn for company around the clock.

"I want to wake up and know that there's someone else in the room. Or at least the next. To wake me up with the sound of the tap running, and to bother me with the sound of his dragging feet in his slippers. To drop his fork and wake me up with a start. To tell me, "turn off that radio, won't you, so I can sleep" and not have it on all night, burning the midnight oil so I can have company..." These little tiny very everyday things that annoyed millions of wives around the world, these were what Meropi missed and asked for. *"Do something, on the off chance a man of my age is found and wants to live together! I'm sick and tired of coming home alone like a willow in the mist!"*

Meropi had confided in the photographer and he felt frustrated. Meropi was withered. Her face was like a geographical relief map. Only her eyes were still full of life and beauty which was clearly visible, still shining brightly. And the soft voice that came out of her sapless lips was her second plus, as were Meropi's good heart and soul. The photograph however couldn't show her good heart or her rich soul, her voice couldn't be printed on paper and that's why the photographer was faced with achieving the impossible. Two grooms came up for Meropi, one from America and one from Australia. It was a gleam of hope when everything else seemed to fade away... Meropi thought of trying her luck even though she believed that all hope for her had long since been abandoned gone.

"*AND NOW, what do we do?*" Vlassis the photographer had wondered and then turned on the spot lights at the studio. He turned Meropi left, he turned her right, he elevated the chair, and he lowered the chair. He threw shadows, he threw light, he dimmed the light, he played *chiaroscuro*[27] with her like a contemporary Caravaggio.

He told her, "*Look this way*", "*Look that way*", "*Do your hair to the back, front, sideways...*" He'd lower the spotlights and then he'd turn them off only to turn them back on again. At last! He had found it! He'd shoot a *profil perdu*[28]. Yes, yes, yes! The *lost* profile was exactly what she needed. Exactly what suited her. The only shot he'd risk taking of her. A *profil perdu* and plenty of shadow. Like mist. When the picture was developed, Meropi pulled a long face.

"*But you can't see anything here! Only my ear is distinguishable and that... merely by the earring! Are you*

---

[27] Italian in text: *light-dark*. A revolutionary technique of painting, a dramatic, sacramental game of contrasts between the light and the shadow; The Italian *post-Renaissance, tenebrist (shadowist)* painter *Michelangelo Merisi da Caravaggio* introduced chiaroscuro and sealed the *Baroque* School of painting.

[28] French in text: *Lost profile*. The artist portrays the head by turning it so far away that the profile of the head is not visible; the only profile outline that is visible is the cheek, and the head is seen from behind *en profil perdu*.

Chapter 8   Look at the birdie.

mocking me, young man, or is it my imagination?"

The photographer persuaded her to show him some trust and blind trust at that! Just like the photo which looked as if it didn't exist. No matter how good one's eyesight was, there would still be difficulty in understanding what it was one was looking at. She trusted him. It was her last chance. And the photos were sent, one to America and one to Australia.

The groom from America didn't reply. He didn't like it, he wasn't convinced by the photo, or he never got the letter and photo, who knows... The groom from Australia though, liked Meropi. He might have found the photo artistic, may also have been happy to take a risk. Meropi married her Greek-Australian.

Everyone back home said: *"Wow, a groom was found for Meropi..? Then, none of the women will remain unwed!"*

The *profil perdu* was what enthralled him, they said.

Meropi got to Australia after a forty-eight-day voyage. She freshened up her face, she tried to preen herself. She saw dark circles under her bright eyes, her face dull from exhaustion. She attempted to go out on deck. Two young, fresh, Greek brides-to-be, passed by her in a hurry.
"I must have gone mad, how am I to compete with them?"
She was disappointed and seriously thought of not getting off the ship but turning back instead.
When she finally disembarked from the *Hellenis* and set foot on the harbor of Melbourne, her eyes alighted on a beautiful little placard on which her name was written in hand printed Greek ΜΕΡΟΠΗ. A man hidden behind a huge bouquet of

red roses was lifting it as high as he a lot could. He wasn't that good looking; he was a wrinkled old man who also looked like the marsupial of the fifth continent. However, he was as taking as they were. Further away, on a small slope, Meropi caught a glimpse of something else.

A number of bouquets made of gorgeous flowers were thrown to the ground. She asked him why. He explained that the voyage was a long one, almost fifty days at sea, which she of course already knew. What she didn't know was that some brides never reached their intended destination to the groom that awaited them, as some of their fellow-travelers often stole their hearts. He stated that he had also experienced this anxiety until he finally saw her coming and Meropi was flattered; she smiled shyly like a child. He was very good with her.

He loved her and looked after her as if she was his own little girl. His sixty-five year old little girl to be exact.

"I felt it again! I feel like a little girl! He made me forget how old I am! Even though what I'm experiencing isn't the reality!" she wrote to her friends in Greece.

A year later, Meropi and her Greek-Australian husband sent the fare for the journey to Vlassis the photographer so that he could visit them. They considered him the key to their happiness. He accepted the invitation. He too settled in Australia so he could *"take pictures of the expatriate Greeks in Australia and the kangaroos!"* as he used to say. He became the community photographer. He ended up marrying the daughter of Meropi's sister-in-law, and they all lived happily ever after.

Chapter 8   Look at the birdie.

Shortly before he migrated though, he had yet another photographic success.

MERSINI also got married because of his photography. Mersini believed that it was him to whom she owed her successful marriage to the fabulous young Greek-Canadian, Croesus to him. The truth of the matter was that Mersini owed all this to her beauty because Mersini wasn't an old woman. She was a beautiful, fresh young filly. Just a month earlier she had graduated from Sixth Form College. She liked school and wished to continue her studies but there was no money. She was a fatherless and her mother worked as a scrubwoman. She had also taken on the washing and ironing of hotel bed sheets. She had three younger siblings who lived in hope of a plate of food and place in the sun.

The idea for Mersini's marriage came from Joan, the American wife of the town. The bridegroom was of Greek origin, but born and raised in Vancouver. His mother was Greek and he had studied at the same college as, Joan's brother, with whom he was friends.

Mersini had gone along for the shoot in borrowed clothes and shoes. Augusta had flung her wardrobe wide open and Mersini chose. They had the same shape of body and wore the same size of shoes. Thirty-seven. Joan had had the same intention of offering to lend Mersini something to wear, but she was taller and wore a larger size in clothes and shoes. I any case, Mersini felt more at ease with Augusta.

She braided her hair in one plait and let it fall over her left shoulder. She didn't need to spend any time preening herself. The photo was filled with youth and freshness. It overflowed with beauty. Two months later, the pretty Greek girl was walking up the aisle in Canada.

"Here, they don't say 'Look at the birdie' nor do they say 'the birdie will come out'. Here, they say, 'Say Cheese' because when you say 'Cheese' your teeth show just as much as they need to for the smile to be broad and pretty, so the picture comes out nicely. Read it, please, to Vlassis so he can learn this just in case he acquires a foreign customer. He'll need it. Or, he can say it to Joan whenever he shoots pictures of her. It will impress her." Mersini wrote to her mother. *"Then again, it will go to his head! Please, don't read him this!"* she wrote.

And so, Vlassis, the man who became the photographer of transatlantic matchmakings renown, knew all about telling his Australian customers to *Say Cheese* well before he travelled to their country! Well before he learnt their language... Because there, they too were also in the habit of saying *Say Cheese*...

Chapter 9   Josephine the black, the white…

THE FIRST DAYS, when he brought her, she seemed like a frightened little animal. An exotic, beautiful, rare little creature, black in color. She would look shyly around, she would try to smile, but she could never achieve it. In the middle of the smile, something always happened, and it either faded away or froze. And it would remain at the stage of a half smile…

Some unexpected stupid loud laugh, some rude, conspiratorial whispers, a nudge with an elbow to the one sitting beside them. And half words. And humour. Black. Just like Dominique.
Because Dominique, the rare creature that everyone quaintly stared at or better still stared strangely at, was also black. She was a beautiful black African, from the southern hemisphere, who had reached the northern, following the man of her dreams and her life, who, unluckily for her, was white. But, unluckily for him too, since he was none other than Kyriakos who, apart from being white, also happened to be Aspasia's - mainly hers- and Vassili's only child.
And Aspasia preferred a white daughter-in-law rather than Dominique who was not… Just as she preferred to fill her vases with forget-me-nots and touch-me-nots and when she found none of these, she preferred them empty… She looked as if she knew what she really wanted but also looked as if she never knew how to retreat, to negotiate, to manoeuvre.

"But… can't you see? She's as black as the ace of spades! Pitch black! This one here, will not leap to the eye at night!" She had started grumbling, after she had embraced her son and extended a cold hand towards poor Dominique who had been staring at all of them in turn, all three of them, either in the mouth -she mainly looked at Aspasia in the mouth, yet,

without fully understanding what she was saying as she was speaking like a mad machine gun which attacks the enemy without letting a bullet go to waste- or the eyes, so that she could guess what they were saying. Dominique knew quite a bit of Greek, however, all of them in there -especially the lady of the house- seemed to speak without taking a breath and she had difficulty in understanding.

"... and what about the teachers? What about my prestige? How will I introduce her to the school, to the teachers, being as black as sin as she is? She can't even be distinguished!"
Aspasia had panicked as she was the Lyceum Headmistress and she feared her associates' opinions.
"Your prestige? Dominique has nothing to do with your prestige! Introduce her during the day time then so she could be seen! Come on, mom! Is that your problem? What the teachers will say? Dominique is a great person, a wonderful girl, and I wouldn't exchange her for ten white women! Despite the fact that she is also pretty! And my fiancée!"
Kyriakos was fighting his corner, embracing Dominique protectively by the shoulders.

"She scares me, child! Aren't you afraid of her? In those nations down there, they still eat each other! And afterwards, they primp their hair with the bones of those they have eaten! And don't talk to me about a fiancée! I don't remember betrothing you or promising you to anyone! And I sent you to France to bring me a degree and not to fetch me a negress! For years I've spent a whole fortune and now... Look at the outcome!" She raised her voice even more and pointed her finger at Dominique -she was the outcome- and now she looked even more frightened.

Chapter 9   Josephine the black, the white...

"*A Negress!*" she added with revulsion. "*I brought a degree, but not for you mom! I got it for me! It may not have been what I wanted, it could be what you have chosen, but... I got it for me! And Dominique, I brought her also for me! Because she appealed to me! You may rest assured that I didn't bring her all the way here only to check out whether she appeals to you! As for her name, well, it's Do-mi-ni-que! Not Nergress! Am I understood, Mom?*"
He sounded bitter and determined not to let his mother have the upper hand, like back then when Kyriakos hadn't
wanted to become a civil engineer, she wanted him to though and so what he wanted made no difference, because she had known her son was destined to be a civil engineer from the moment she'd given birth to him and because everything in the family always happened the way she wanted. She felt herself to be powerful and so she imposed herself. All the others, within or outside the family, relatives, friends and acquaintances knew that she was ill-mannered due to her obstinacy. And these were traits of her personality that she'd carried with her since childhood and she neither wanted nor tried to get rid of them or make them better. However, now, the time had come to change a few things and she sensed it. Kyriakos was obviously determined and she saw it... And she didn't like it at all.

"*And... what sort of children will you bear Kyriakos, dear? White or black*", she tried to find a good, palpable reason so that she could perturb her son and thus have her way once more. If he had written to tell her at least before he came, that Dominique, the woman that he had blurted out about a year ago that he was in love with, was black, she would have found something to toss up...

"Well, black-white mum! Some kindness even if you don't have any? I would really appreciate it, you know!"

"Kindness, I've got! Understanding don't expect me to have because that ran out as soon as you arrived! Because the children that you will bear, will be black! Pitch black! Just like their mother! And in order to wed them, you'll have to take them there, far away, to Jim Crow land! Because here, no one will ever be found to wed them!" Now, Aspasia was howling. The machine gun was delivering a broadside.

"With all due respect, but, where do you live, mom? In what planet? Haven't you learnt anything from the many trips you have taken in Europe and America? From all the conferences you've been to and the books you've read? You are, really, unbelievable!" Kyriakos, obviously disappointed, pulled Dominique closer to him.

"You, what's wrong with you Vassilis? Has the cat got your tongue? Or maybe you also like the negress? Say something! You're his father! Is this why you raised him? So a negress can snatch him away from you?" she leashed out at her husband, who may indeed not have anticipated a black bride for his son, he may also not have been very enthusiastic in the way that all this had emerged, not only unexpectedly but also black, but he did however have, the decency and maturity, the self-restraint and the kindness not to show it.

Chapter 9   Josephine the black, the white...

For Vassilis, Kyriakos was above all, their only child, and this was something Vassilis didn't seem to forget. He neither wanted to put him down in front of Dominique nor upset him by offending her, knowing that she was important to him, not to mention the fact that she was amiable and charming. And now, the way that she cringed beside his son, frightened and ill-at-ease, he couldn't find the heart to see anything of what Aspasia saw.

HE ONLY SAW two Kyriakos in front of him today. The child who, years before, loved to climb on his father's back and with his tiny hands in his father's palms stretched above him, would say: "*Look! I will be this tall when I grow up!*" and the grown up, tall Kyriakos, who now like a proper man, defended the girl he loved. Defended her against his own parents, in his own home... "*But... are we strangers? Or maybe his enemies? He has come to announce a formal decision concerning his life from now on and my boy has to apologize for that?*" he thought to himself, deeply touched and disappointed by his wife's multiple attacks.

"*I... what can I say! Dominique, bienvenue a la famille!*[29] *Bienvenue! She seems like a good girl! She must be for her to have been with our Kyriakos three years now, isn't that what you said Kyriakos? He must love her and she must be worth it! Hmm, she's black! What do you suggest, Aspasia? Making her white? It's more important to be kind in heart and soul. And in manners. She seems like a fine girl to me! If Kyriakos wants her, we have no say in this Aspasia! He is not a child... Let alone that now there will be three civil*

---

[29] French in text: "*Welcome to family! Welcome!*"

engineers in the family! You see, she's also a civil engineer! A hard working girl! Dominique, ma femme est bonne, mais elle aime beaucoup notre fils. Tu as compris? Elle croit qu'il est encore petit! Mais, il n'y a pas de probleme! D'accord?"[30] Vassilis had tried to patch things up, as always, and this sudden misfortune, called Dominique, had taken them or actually had taken Aspasia by surprise. As a sober adult and good father, he tried to make things look better in his wife's eyes and Dominique, at last, smiled.

"Are you crazy? You agree to this? Instead of telling him: 'My child, have all the white women disappeared?' You urge him on?"

"Listen Aspasia, I studied in Germany, you know that... So I know what it's like to be stared at with a scowl just because you're foreign! Just because you aren't one of them! Only because of that! Even if you are even better than them! I know what that decent old lady, Frau Gertraud, went through when her grandson, Wolfgang, returned and asked me way past midnight to empty the room! He shouted that if he had known that the lodger in the attic, meaning me, was a foreigner and not a German, he would have never have allowed his grandmother to rent it. He didn't want anything to do with foreigners, he said. His grandmother though, an educated and kind lady, not only managed to let me stay, but also got her grandson to apologize the very next day. Yes, Kyriakos, I am talking about the very same Wolfgang, the one who has become my friend...

---

[30] French in text: *"My wife is a good person, but she loves our son very much. Do you understand? She believes he is still a little boy! But it isn't a problem! Do you agree?"*

Chapter 9   Josephine the black, the white...

So, Aspasia, if you had ever had such incidents happen to you, undoubtedly now, you wouldn't be looking at what color Dominique is! Do you understand? Come on! You have scared the wits out of the girl! Look at how she's staring at you!" Vassilis explained and patted his son and Dominique on the back in a friendly way.

"Thank you, father!"

"Well, right now I've really got it coming from your mother! I just ensured myself a good dose of curtain lecture!" Vassilis joked and Aspasia burst into tears like an enfant gâté[31], running towards the kitchen and forcefully slamming the door behind her. The rest of them, just looked at each other. Josephine got them out of their awkward predicament.

AUGUSTA had brought her there just like every Wednesday evening. For years now, Wednesday evenings were evenings of children's literature for Aspasia and Josephine. Aspasia read aloud fairy tales to Josephine in English and French and translated as well. She also made her plum pudding with walnuts from a recipe she had got from a restaurant in London.

However, Dominique, the bride that wasn't white, had made her forget all about their literature evening and Josephine who had shrunk into a corner between the secretaire and the bookcase, graveled about her older friend's outbursts. She had seen the entire welcoming scene. Dominique was gorgeous. Tall, with a beautiful figure. She also had pretty eyes. They were sad, however, and on the verge of tears -

---

[31] French in text: *"spoiled child"*

maybe it was Aspasia's fault... Her hair had a bunch of small, tiny curls, "*innumerable*" she thought. She hadn't understood why Aspasia didn't want her... maybe because she had been talking non-stop, at a stretch. She was glad that Kyriako had stood up for Dominique -and what a handsome young man he had become. And she was also glad when his father had said that he wanted Dominique, too. In the end, however, Aspasia had burst into tears and Josephine was afraid that Dominique would do the same and she almost anticipated it.

And now, that the lady of the house had left without mentioning whether they'd let Dominique to stay or not -nor her, because of the way she had been left forgotten for so long. Neither did she know what would become of the plum pudding with the walnuts which smelt delicious and the little girl was now afraid that in the end, the pudding would surely cook to a cinder -just like the time when Lela had burnt one of their cakes because she had been chatting with the neighbors.

She sneezed. They all turned towards her. Saw her. Remembered her.

"*Josephine, my child, did we forget you?*" said Vassilis.

"*Who is this young lady? Josephine? Dear me! How you have grown since the summer when I took my leave of you! Come, let me introduce you to Dominique!*" said Kyriakos.

"*How are you? I am Dominique!*"

"*So I've heard! You are beautiful! Why doesn't Mrs. Aspasia want you? What have you done to her?*" she innocently asked.

Chapter 9   Josephine the black, the white...

"I want her! Of course, I want her! Even if I didn't want her to start with, I shall, my dear child, since my son pulled this off very well!" the hostess interjected. She had returned quietly, quite unlike that loud exit of hers a while earlier. She was holding a platter with the pudding and she had surely freshened up.

"When did she ever find the time?" Vassilis admired her.

"Is that for us, mom?" asked Kyriakos.

"No, it's for me, but you can have some! It's Wednesday's plum pudding!" Josephine cut in.

"What pudding could I have made for you? Did I even know that you'd be coming? I thought you were in Paris! You said that you'd be coming next month and you showed up like a comet! With one surprise after another! You didn't even want us at the airport this time! You see, you had someone today to help you with your luggage!" Aspasia continued to whine and Kyriako sweetly hushed her *Ssssh!!* She shook her head and for a minute it seemed that she would hush, but she didn't.

Then, two books from the *"Lilika"* series which Josephine had in her arms, fell down on the floor. Dominique helped Josephine to pick them up from the floor.

"Qu' est-ceque c'est?" [32] said Dominique.
"Oh la la! It is Martine!"
"No, it is Lilika!" Josephine sounded certain.

---
[32] *French in text: "What is this?"*

Dominique knelt next to her and explained that the original series were French and the little hero was none than *Martine*; but after being translated into Greek, they had made it *Lilika*. She also said that she was personally acquainted with Monsieur Marcel Marlier, the painter of *Martine* or *Lilika*, as well as of all the illustrations of the series. She promised that the next time she visited Paris she would bring back for Josephine two of the latest books signed by both the author and the painter.

Aspasia, who was looking at Dominique, was excited. Dominique was approaching the little girl tenderly and elegantly; she was using the Greek language in a clever way and above all, yes, she seemed to have many virtues and that was exactly what was scaring Aspasia because she had to accept them! No, Aspasia was not going to give up in front of Dominique! Never!

"Did you, my boy, teach her to say "How are you? I am Dominique!" Was it you?"

"Me, mom, but also on her own, so she could communicate with all of you. So we can all have a better time. She speaks Greek quite well and she understands even more. And everything you have said, here, tonight, she has understood almost all of it... Dominique is determined to stay here, mom, and she will because I want her to! Do you understand?"

"And what sort of wedding will you have, darling? With tom-toms in the jungle? With the in laws dancing around a huge pot, yowling? Dominique, you answer me, since you understand everything!" she was sure that she hadn't understood a word of what was being said.

Chapter 9   Josephine the black, the white...

"Madam, I am Chrisdian! In church de wedding will be!" she disappointed her, silencing her kindly and proving that she indeed understood everything they said.

"All right! How many languages does this one here speak?" Aspasia admired her.

"Française, English, Spanish, Afrikans, Zoulou, of course, and now, a lit-tle Gre-ek, Ma-dam ! »

"Zoulou? Oh my God ! She... said... she... speaks... Zoulou... of c o u r s e... if she speaks Zoulou... ohhh... then it means that..." Aspasia was really scared but fortunately, Josephine's declaration interrupted her.

"When I grow up, I want to be like Dominique! Tall and beautiful with many languages and... black!"

" My sweet little girl, you scare me... really! Of course looks better that you decided not to follow Akka of Kebnekaise and her flock and fly with them above their country! But, I also remember that a short while ago, you wanted to become Japanese, like Keiko! Last year, you wanted to be an American, like Joan! Now you want to blacken? But, aren't you happy, child, that you're white?" Aspasia was about to flub it again.

"I like it that I'm white! Just like the "saumon" silken flosses that Lela uses to embroider the faces on her embroidery, but I also really like Joan and Keiko and this one here... ooh, I've forgotten her name!" and Kyriakos reminded her... "Yes, I really like Dominique! And she looks like chocolate! I don't care at all that she's black, and neither should you and Mrs. Aspasia shouldn't cry because Dominique is black! Look! Not *even she is crying even though she is! And when I grow up, I want to be for a little while, American and black and Japanese with slanted eyes but in the end I want to be white again, what I mean is "saumon", so that my mom won't also end up crying -as Mrs. Aspasia did- because I am black!"*

"So, you're going to be something like Josephine, the white, the black, the yellow and the red?" Kyriakos joked.

"Yes, that's exactly who I'll be! And if Mrs. Aspasia doesn't want your wife, because she's black, we'll take her to our home, since we want her! We want everybody!"

"We'll keep her, dear child! We want her! Don't you worry! Dominique will stay here until they build their own house and then she can live with Kyriakos. Because I would never live in the same house with my daughter-in-law, even if she were white!" She reassured her and went on without caring that she was being heard. *"How fortunate it is that mama*

Chapter 9   Josephine the black, the white...

Grammatiki, my mother, isn't alive to taste this cup of sorrow! Even though now she's surely turning in her grave! How could she ever imagine that she'd have black great grandchildren! What degree of black? Pitch black to be exact!" -

"Mom!" Kyriakos shouted at her.

"What? If I want to be on good terms with my child, I have to accept Dominique and not speak my mind? To dance to your tunes, yours and hers? I don't know if I can perform miracles, but for your sake, my son, I'll try! I say! She learnt Greek and namely for Kyriako! And for us! You seem very intelligent to me, Dominique! Who knows, God may have made you black, but maybe he made you that way for Kyriako's own good in the end..." Aspasia always appreciated intelligent people who had some good way to show their intelligence.

And this one here, the unforeseen Dominique, certainly seemed to display plenty of that and it had attracted her attention. All of a sudden, she wanted her, not to disappear before her eyes as she wanted it to as soon as she saw her pass over the threshold with her son but to learn everything about her.

"Now Dominique, please, come here, sit down by me -she offered her the two seater couch- *and tell me about yourself. Where exactly do you come from? Have you any siblings? Parents? Do they know you are here? And if so, have they given permission? What work do they do? Do they live in Paris or in Africa?..."*

"Mom, you forgot the lamp!" Kyriakos laughed.

"The lamp? What lamp?"

"Well, how will you interrogate her without a lamp?" joked Kyriakos who sensed that sooner or later his mother would take to Dominique. With a little luck also, maybe she would love her, too.

"She seems so gentle... surely she's had a good upbringing, it's something which shows... And so, apart from my Kyriakos, she might not have anyone else in this hemi-sphere... she seems a very sweet girl, her good manners are evident, it can't be denied... Maybe I was a bit hasty when I became angry on seeing her come in; And now, how can I make up for it? Without of course, letting her upstage me!"
Aspasia thought all this but never expressed it out loud, to anyone. Not even to Vassilis, who she confided in about everything...

DOMINIQUE came out of her shell very quickly. She was helped in doing so, not only by Kyriakos but also Aspasia who appraised her correctly and believed in her. Instead of causing her problems, she respected and brought her out, she protected and praised her.

"Who could ever have imagined that I would become the guardian angel of a negress and that I would love her on top of it all! Because I do love that gal" she confessed to Vassili and he had told her that he had been certain that it would turn out this way, *"because you're as sweet as sugar and as bitter as poison..."*

At the wedding, the African in-laws from Cote d' Ivoir weren't wearing bones in their hair. Neither did they eat anybody. Nor did they dance around a huge pot. They had come with

Chapter 9   Josephine the black, the white...

their women and children from their country -thirty two people in all- and all of them were quite civilized and very well mannered. Aspasia welcomed them and she was a first class hostess and when the mother of Dominique said that she entrusted her daughter to Kyriakos and his family and she wants them to love her, then Aspasia greatly surprised them all as she cried, putting Dominique in her lap, holding her tightly and declaring in front of all:

"I've loved Dominique from the first moment I met her! But, the truth is that I didn't want to accept this... and even now... I don't really know why... And it may have been Kyriakos who brought her home, but it was Me who made her part of the family!" Aspasia, as always, wanted to have the final word, whatever it was.

Anyway, the truth is that her heart had really been softened and it had all begun when she had seen Dominique kneeling on the floor helping Josephine to gather up her books from the *Lilika* or *Martine* series -it made little difference which...

The grandchildren that Dominique gave her were twins and according to their grandmother's predictions, dark in colour. Not pitch black nor as black as the ace of spades but they had the sweetest brown colour of milk chocolate and Kyriakos' characteristics in their features. Aspasia called them *my chocolates* and *my piccanninies* and of course she adored them. The baby girl turned out to be a real nagger *"a spitting image of her grandma, Aspasia..."*
Kyriakos teased her but she couldn't care less.

JOSEPHINA was a skinny child. Most the neighborhood children were chubby and some of them were downright fat, and they had huge cheeks! Juicy, plump and pitch red! The truth of the matter was that she was a very healthy child despite her thinness. She rarely got ill and when she did, it was only because she had contracted a childhood's disease or she happened to come down with a cold. But even then, there was a slight temperature, a slight cough and that was all. She always got better well before the doctor's expectancies and way beyond them. Lela, however, didn't see any plump cheeks and so couldn't accept the fact that Josephina, who as a baby had been plump, all of a sudden was no longer so! Let alone that the nursery song "the white and *chubby little lamb, its mother full of pride...*" kept going on round and round in her head and she'd sing it to Josephina in order to make her eat and the little one would retort each time, *"Well I am not a lamb, so there's no reason for me being white and chubby!"* and then Lela would frown...

So, there was no getting out of Lela's head, not for a minute, the idea that she had to plumpen her up, yet she didn't know how to do it and kept looking for a way.

Without a word to anybody, she decided to take her to Old Voula. She arranged everything and the appointment was made. Old Voula lived on the ground floor of an imposing, huge old two storey mansion-house. The house was vast and the ground floor was more than enough for her now that she had been left all alone, she'd say. Her children had scattered to the four corners of the earth. One was an ambassador, another was a consul and the other was a military attaché somewhere abroad. Her daughter taught ballet at the dance

Chapter 10   Old Voula.

school run by her French husband, somewhere in France. They'd all meet up, all four of them with their families, at their mother's home every Christmas, Easter and almost all the summer. Only then or on some celebration did she open up the second floor of the house which she kept locked up the rest of the year. Only then from both floors of Old Voula's home, did voices overflow... the voices of all eleven grandchildren which had been given to her by her three sons and one daughter.

They crossed the big garden, walking underneath the palm trees. Twelve enormous palm trees in two lines, framed the central pathway. The stone flower beds on either side didn't look untended but neither did they look very well-kept. Most of them needed trimming. Lela rapped on the door with the knocker, which was a beautiful, bronze, woman's hand. Everything had been arranged in the way Old Voula had specified.

The moon had just come out and it was full. Mario was at work and Augusta was lying in bed reading. Everything was exactly how it was supposed to be. Lela had told them that she would be visiting an aunt of hers and had asked to take Josephina for company.
On the way, she explained to Josephina that she had to behave herself and do exactly what she was told to by a *"nice granny who loves children and makes them brisken"*.
"Brisken? What is brisken?" The little one had wondered.

"To be... be... be strong! Yes that's it! To be strong" Lela had explained.

OLD VOULA welcomed them, drying her dripping hands on

her checkered apron which she had tied around her waist. Then, the front door clicked shut behind them because as the hostess said, there was a draft blowing through from the open kitchen door, which led to the back yard. She led them to the inside of the house. They walked behind her, through a very long hallway, which divided the ground floor in two. It resembled a hospital corridor and it had stark portraits on the walls on the right and left between the doors. The doors numbered about a dozen, all wooden and painted lilac. The hallway seemed to be endless but they finally reached the end. The kitchen was there with the pervasive smell of spices. It smelt of a bit of everything. Cinnamon and vanilla, nutmeg and saffron, Guinea pepper and tea, chamomile and laurel, rosemary, peppermint and oregano.

She had three built in fire baskets for cooking and pretty tiles on the floor which formed a black and white chess board. Blackish smith's pliers were hanging in front of the fire baskets. Strings of garlic, chili peppers, corn, rosemary, lavender and peppermint, were hanging from the wooden beams of the ceiling. Well polished, copper pots, which shone in the light of the candles, hung on the walls alongside pretty moulds for cakes, charlotte puddings, some with intricate designs, carved fruit and flowers; all of them in copper. Old Voula was having a hard time untying her apron and asked for Lela's help.

"Without an apron, I can do no chores", she explained. *"Of course, everything is done by Urania but I do wash my up glass every once in a while!"*

There were some weird things on top of a wooden worktop. Lela seemed to identify them immediately. She had surely

Chapter 10   Old Voula.

seen them before. Old Voula had it all down to a fine art. She was good at what she did, even though she wasn't a professional. Even though she never took money, not a dime, to be exact! She had all the money she needed anyway, handed down through the generations. Money and glory. Her grandfathers were squires and her father and husband were top ranking military men.

In a built-in adjunct of the hallway, beside one of those closed doors, a floor pillow covered with the Greek flag had all of her father's medals on while a second one in white satin had all of her husband's.

That's why whatever that old woman did was done solely for the people's well-being, for the souls of her mother and father and for that of her late husband. Not forgetting, of course, for her own.

A third kitchen door opened and an extremely short woman came in. Josephina felt scared. The short woman was only about an inch taller than herself. She was certainly very old. She had grey hair, woven in a very long braid which reached down to below her knees.

"An old goblin!" The little girl was terrified. Her eyes weren't straight; one was bigger than the other and they looked in different directions. She had a congenial smile, however, and so Josephina relaxed somewhat. The short woman said *"good evening"* with a smile and asked Old Voula, whom she reached only to waist height, if she could be of any help. Old Voula showed her the little sticks on the worktop. Then, turning to Josephina, because Lela seemed to know the short woman, she said:

"This is Urania! She is my mother's fosterling! She is the one who raised me! The only thing she didn't do was breastfeed me! Urania was part of my dowry! We are going to die together, us two... we've grown used to each other" and smiled.

Urania, who was obviously a dwarf, nodded her head with a smile, again, and took an oblong white enamel box in her hands, much like the one doctors have in their surgeries and place their tongs and pliers inside. It also contained those strange small sticks.

Josephine was still muddling up her counting a little and so didn't manage to correctly count all those long sticks which looked like the wooden skewers used for *souvlaki*. These sticks however had both sides firmly wrapped in cotton. This resulted in them looking a bit like the sticks the priest used in church for the Extreme Unction of Passion Week. There was also a jar of honey on that same work pot, not that she saw it, but she did hear Old Voula saying *"bring me the honey, too"* to Urania and she gave her a tin gallipots. Following that, Urania stood beside Old Voula, in the middle of the kitchen, beside the huge square table with its wicker chairs, holding the sticks in the one hand and the honey in the other and she yawned closing her eyes. Old Voula continuously threw jovial smiles at Lela and the child while ferreting about in the table drawer searching for something. Lela returned the smiles. Josephina did not. Everything was strange and frightening. The house, Old Voula and that short woman who was so troll-like!

Josephina had once met Apostolaki in Athens, a gnomish, little man just like this one here, Urania. He didn't scare her

Chapter 10   Old Voula.

though. He wasn't old and wrinkled like this short one here. Neither did he have an enormous braid trailing behind him as if it were his tail! Nor had she met him in dusky light! Old Voula's kitchen was gloomy as it was only illuminated by an oil lamp on the wall and a small vigil candle on the worktop beside the kitchen sink. Beyond the two or three short chunk candles on the bench beneath the wall with the copper casing, a single oil-lamp shone on the opposite wall, next to the picture of the Virgin Mary who held Christ her child in her arms, when he was small; and a small oil-lamp on the bench next to the sink, of the type which grandmothers tend to light for the *spirits* in the evenings. The four walls of the kitchen were full of dreadful, wobbling shadows.

She looked at the faces again, one by one. Lela was smiling in contentment. Josephina didn't know why. Old Voula seemed to be on the point of doing something; it was anyone's guess what. Urania, like a loyal dog, waited for Old Voula's command. And the silence... which was also like a face and it could also be seen. Josephina saw it everywhere. She could touch it! It was a queer silence which wouldn't break even when someone spoke maybe because all of them had spoken in soft, whispering voices. The silence wasn't broken, not even when Old Voula opened the squeaking drawer of the table, nor when she slammed it shut and said that it needed oiling.

Josephina was a fearless child; they all knew that. Tonight however, she felt ill at ease... strange... She felt inhibitions she had never felt before... inhibitions which she never knew existed. She could feel that something strange was going on... something which purely out of instinct, she didn't want to find out.

The two women, Old Voula and Urania the goblin, told her to keep her body straight and still. She looked at Lela, who gestured with her eyes and head to do so. Urania lifted her coatee and t-shirt up to her nape. A hand went up and down her spine, touching the tender backbone which writhed under the frozen hand.

Old Voula started murmuring under her breath but Josephina couldn't make out what she said. The words seemed to be in a disjointed order whenever they managed to come out whole, between her murmurs. Words like *"moon"*, *"waxing"*, *"illness"*, *"evil eye"*, *"Virgin* Mary", *"brisken"* and *"brisken"* again and *"Virgin Mary"* again and *"moon"* again but *"silver"* this time. She murmured and dipped the ends of her sticks inside the honey.

Then she'd touch each vertebra on Josephina's back one by one, starting from the nape. She'd then leave the used stick and get a new one only to start over again, dipping it in honey and spreading it on each vertebra, always murmuring.

Josephina shivered at every touch. She was disgusted by the honeyed cotton that touched her skin. Somewhere between the fifth and sixth stick, she couldn't take it anymore. She abruptly got up and moved away, startling all three of them. Old Voula cut her murmuring short, and angrily looked at her, abandoning her smiles for the first time. Josephina arched her back and shoulders as if they had thrown cold water on her and shivered again.

"I don't want anymore! I am leaving! I want my mom!" She was angry and was fiercely addressing Lela. Old Voula and the short woman tried in vain to persuade her that the *"remedy"* couldn't be left half finished.

Chapter 10   Old Voula.

"Let her finish it off so you can brisken!" Lela told her.

"What a pity! There goes tonight... It's as if it never happened! Now, we have to wait until next month, in the waxing of the moon! Dear child, if only you knew what you were doing! A whole month gone to waste" Old Voula explained, smiling again.

"And for how many waxing gibbous moons will I have to bring her, aunt Voula?" Lela asked disappointed.

"We'll have to see about that! When the child starts to "wax", we'll know! You will see it yourself. She will strengthen up! She'll gain weight. Some need about five full moons, others two and others ten! What else can I tell you? We'll see!" Old Voula answered with the air of a professional.

The little girl didn't even say good bye on leaving even though they both held out their hand and refused to take the pancakes with cinnamon, honey and nuts that Urania offered her. Lela could barely hold her. She was clutching her little hand hard, she knew it, but if she loosened it just a bit, the little one would run away and that wasn't allowed to happen. Lela felt gratitude for Old Voula and shame on behalf of Josephina, who had cut short the *remedy* half finished. She leaned and kissed Old Voula's hand and only then did she decide to leave, apologizing for the hundredth time.

As soon as they got outside Old Voula's gate, Lela scolded the child.

"I brought you for your own good and you have made a fool of me! You are all bones and I felt sorry for you! That's why I brought you here, to gain strength and be plump like all

the other children! Some of them are chubby and they have nothing to eat! And you have all the goodies in the world and you are all skin and bones! It's my fault! Mine alone, for caring about you!"

Josephina looked as if she hadn't heard a word. She had her mouth clamped tight shut and she was steaming in anger.

It was back at home where all hell broke loose. As soon as they opened the gate, she ran to the front door and started banging on the doorknob until Augusta came out, disturbed. She darted inside and ran up the stairs. Augusta followed her, but couldn't understand what was going on. Josephina went into the bathroom and was taking off her little clothes one by one after having first turned on the hot water tap, which started steaming.

"Mummy, mom! I am never again going to that old woman with the mustaches! She was like a witch! ...and Lela allowed her to spread honey on me! They said that she'd have to take me there again! I am not going! The short one was there, too! Short like Apostolakis who we find in the streets of Athens and while Apostolakis is good, this one here is not!" Josephina tried to explain through her tears. Augusta, who was stupefied, was picking her clothes up from the floor. She suddenly turned around and saw Lela crossing herself, looking up at the heavens, in an attempt to catch the Lord's attention so he would help get her out of this difficult situation. Augusta angrily asked for explanations.

"Who did you take the child to? What the hell is going on here? What old woman is she talking about? And what business was it of Apostolakis to come all the way here?

Chapter 10   Old Voula.

What is this honey that they spread on her? Who spread it? Speak!"

Josephina was sinking into the tub, sobbing her heart out. Lela started to speak and she was even more upset and poised to explain; *"...anyway I don't know this... this... Apostolakis you're talking about! This is the first time I've ever heard of him! I don't even know the quality of honey they smeared the child with but anyway it would be good... perhaps... I don't know..."* She went on about the idea she had had to take Josephina to Old Voula so she would be *cured* -although she was not ill- because whoever had skinny children went to Old Voula and after four to five full moons the children gained weight and briskened. And those who never saw any results from the doctors took their children to Old Voula and they got better. Even Lela had been taken to Old Voula when she was little and from then on she had briskened and gained weight.

"And who has told you that she needs to brisken? Why? Is she sick? My child is just fine! Dear Lord, I am going mad! An old woman spreading honey on my child and me having no idea? That's unheard of! It's terrible! In what world are we living, Lela? Let's do away with all the doctors and let's all go to your old woman! Have you gone completely mad? What has gotten into you? I say! The child taken to that old witch for a cure! I want her just the way she is! SKINNY!"

"All right then! She's your child, do whatever you want with her! Josephina, though, is so skinny that her bones can be counted one by one! I see all the other children in the neighborhood, with their chubby little cheeks!" She filled her mouth with air so her cheeks inflated. *"And yours looks like*

she hasn't been fed for ages! Old Voula is the daughter of a general. And her husband was a general, too! She only does good to people, without accepting payment because she has the gift which she got from her mother and she in turn from her grandmother! Old Voula doesn't need money! See! You say that she is a witch and that's why I didn't say anything to you! You always mock everything! I cherish our child, the only thing I didn't do was give birth to her!" she said pointing to Josephine and grabbed one of the towels hanging from the rail and started wiping her eyes with it.

"Whoever heard of honey on the back!" retorted Augusta shivering and continued... *"Take heed of what I'm saying, once and for all! If you want us to go on together, you'll never ever do anything again without asking me first! You are never to take the child anywhere without my knowing exactly where you are taking her to! Understood? And remember: I want my child the way it is, SKINNY! Understood?"* Lela nodded her head in consent.

"The short one had a mustache! They both had mustaches! The tall old woman had these teeth that wagged from side to side whenever she spoke! And she spread stuff on me! She also had a thick braid wrapped around her head! The short one had a tail! A real one! A long one!" whimpered Josephina, who had mistaken Urania's long braid for a tail in the dim light of the kitchen. And she went on, lowering her voice as if she were afraid of being heard, *"She was a goblin! A real troll!"*

Augusta's eyes opened wide and she stared at Lela, waiting for a reasonable explanation.

Chapter 10   Old Voula.

"*Not quite! Urania is a person! It's impossible that she would have a tail! She has a long braid! She hasn't had a hair cut in twenty years, she says! Not a tail!*" Lela answered, looking very disappointedly at Josephina.

Later on, Mario saw the funny side of the whole situation instead of getting angry. "*Bravo, our daughter is very observant! Braids, teeth tails, she saw the whole lot! Come now, calm down and tomorrow morning I'll have a word with Lela.*"

Augusta forbade it, telling him that she didn't feel he was the right person to do so, and that she would handle this matter herself because Lela, whatever she may have done now, was sensitive and if they hurt or insulted her, they may end up making her miserable.

THE FOLLOWING month, Josephina got sick. She had a high fever. Her throat was sore, on both sides, and it hurt. "Mumps" said the doctor who had called on her twice daily for the first two days. On the night of the third day, he came again. Her condition remained unchanged. Mario saw him out to the gate. Augusta sat in the armchair, beside the sick child's bed, waiting for her temperature to fall. It always fell a few degrees after the antipyretic. Mario went down to the ground floor and poked the fire in the fireplace which was about to go out. He picked up a newspaper and tried to read. He didn't succeed. Sleep caught up with him within the first few lines.

That's what Lela wanted. To ensure that Augusta wouldn't ask for her, she fetched the square stool for her legs. She was also on the point of falling asleep as a result of all the worries and the adversity. She wrapped herself in a knitted, woolen shawl. She walked barefoot; crossed the entire ground floor with her shoes in hand. She went outside through the back door and went into the garden, holding the bell's tongue which was hanging from the door, so as not to be heard. Only when she was out on the pavement did she put on her shoes. She started running as if she were being chased after she had thrown one last glance over her shoulder. She was running on the path, parallel to the train tracks. A dog from the other side started barking furiously.

"It took me for an intruder" she thought. Further down was Kassiani's house. There, she stopped running. She walked across the front of it reciting the *Lord's Prayer*. They said it was haunted. Lela believed it but that didn't stop her. She got to the forbidden house; the house of Old Voula.

Chapter 11   The mumps.

The old woman came out on to the threshold in a white wrinkled petticoat which she probably wore as a nightgown. She had her hair loose. It reached down her back. She was yawning. Lela started to tell her something, trying to catch her breath. Old Voula listened to her as she spoke in a low voice, hurriedly and conspiratorially, braiding half her hair cursorily with the speed of a machine as she did so. It was obvious that she didn't like Lela seeing her with loose hair. She thought it was improper.

Lela kept on talking, swinging her arms in movements that showed despair. As soon as Old Voula had braided half her hair, she took out of her bosom a white, hair band which was wrinkled likewise, and tied her braid with it. She started braiding the other half at the same speed. Before she finished, she nodded to Lela to follow her inside the house. She pointed out a flowered sofa at the beginning of the big hallway and told her to sit there. She herself vanished at the end of the hallway, into the kitchen.

She took a long time in there. It took her almost an hour to come back out. It crossed Lela's mind that something had happened to the old woman, or that she might have fallen asleep. She went up and down the dim hallway twice, walking underneath the portraits of the family's long departed ancestors, with their forbidding glares which seemed to be inspecting her and this scared her so she went and stood outside the kitchen door in an attempt to hear or see something through the keyhole. Only several metallic sounds could be rhythmically heard as if something was being stirred. She couldn't see a thing through the keyhole. Only the brick wall opposite could be seen and old Voula passing by twice but so quickly that it looked as if only her petticoat passed by. There was movement in there and that was good.

"*At least the old woman hasn't fallen asleep*" she thought.

It seemed as if centuries passed by, not only moments. Lela shivered at the thought that Augusta or Mario might be searching for her. An old ancient, rickety grandfather clock, which stood somewhere in the middle of the hallway and looked like a war memorial in that imposing wooden frame, struck the time. She got a fright again. She remembered what the old men said. That supposedly old Voula's house was built on top of an ancient cemetery. She shivered. Every strike of the clock had a hollow echo. The eleven times it struck, seemed to sound like twenty-two. At that moment the kitchen door finally opened. Old Voula came out holding something.

A parcel, wrapped in a blue and white, checkered kitchen towel. It looked chubby, rather like the shape and size of the bible, or at least that's how it looked to Lela. The old woman explained something briefly.

They were the "*operating instructions*". She thanked old Voula, who now stood before her yawning incessantly with her wide open toothless mouth, and that's when Lela emembered how frightened Josephina had become the other day, on seeing that mouth wide open.

"*A true noblewoman and she has no teeth! I wonder why?*" Lela wondered despite her haste.

SHE LEFT as hurriedly as she had come, running, after she had asked the old woman "*is that what smells?*" turning towards the open kitchen from where the strange smell was

Chapter 11   The mumps.

emanating from. The old woman replied that it was indeed what smelled like that. She was running but was also being careful so she wouldn't fall and drop the seemingly precious, contents of the parcel. She held it in her arms protectively as if it were a baby. It was warm, or to be more accurate actually it was scorching hot! She took off her shawl even though she was cold. She wrapped the parcel up in it so that her hands and chest wouldn't burn. She went into the garden on tiptoe, after she had taken her shoes off again. With the same caution as she had left, she entered the house and leaving her shoes in the kitchen, she went upstairs to the bedrooms. She carefully unfolded the shawl and the little towel and removed the parcel, just outside Josephina's room.

She opened the little white enamel box that the old woman had given her. There were two circular pieces of wax paper inside, on which was spread a thick layer of a black substance. It smelled strange and steamed. Both pieces were as hot as the small, enamel box. She touched it with her finger. It was sticky. The old woman had told her that it was tar.

"It's the number one remedy for the mumps" Lela thought. And she remembered that her mother had also tarred her, on the right and left side of her throat, where the swelling from the mumps was. Back then, when she was little and she had also contracted that devious childhood disease. And she had recovered, without a doctor or a pharmacist. Using only Old Voula's tar. She carefully took one of the wax papers in her hand, took a deep breath and then, held it, and strode through the door. Augusta was sleeping and so was the patient. She carefully placed the wax paper on the side where the tar was spread, on the right hand side of Josephina's

throat; her heart feeling as if it was about to burst. She didn't have time to press a second time so it could stick better. The little girls screamed in fright. Lela, also startled, took a step back while Augusta shot up from the armchair she had been sleeping in, nearly knocking over the bedside lamp. Within seconds, Mario came rushing into the room tripping on his way.

Josephina was standing up on her quilt, holding her throat with her little hands, making faces full of pain, and refusing to allow Augusta to take her in her arms. All three pairs of eyes, quickly darted to Lela who, being so frightened, instead of making the little box disappear had taken up the second piece of tarred wax paper in her hands. That smell reminded the child's parents of something; it smelled familiar. The shock of the moment though didn't allow for further ascertainment. Josephina was holding in her hands the wax paper which hadn't had time to stick properly on her throat. She looked at it for a few seconds and then threw it in disgust to the floor, shouting that it burnt and stuck like glue. And she was right. She had to shake her hand two or three times to free herself of it.

"What have you done to her? What in the world is this?" Augusta cried out first and grabbed the second circular piece of wax paper from Lela's hand. Mario leaned over so he could have a better look. Then he also yelled.

"Dear Lord! It's tar! How could you? What has she done to you to deserve this?" He shouted angrily and shook her by the shoulders.

"It's tar for the mumps! That's the only way she will get

Chapter 11   The mumps.

better! Otherwise she will burn up with fever!"

"Ohh... no!!!! Well...OK... you are crazy! Downright insane! Certifiable I'd say! Have you gone completely mad?" Augusta went on.

Mario had persuaded Josephina to nest in his arms and was caressing her hair. She was drying her tears and sighing. Then Augusta gestured to Josephina to get back into her bed. The little one obeyed, looking askance at Lela, frightened. Mario called Lela downstairs to have a talk. He sounded stricter than ever. Josephina had finally fallen fast asleep again, with her brownish teddy bear in her arms. Then Augusta also went downstairs.

"What Old Voula and hokum is this? What tar and nostrums? Is Voula a doctor? Tell me!! Is she? Then we shall not go to the other doctors. We should all go to Voula, the old quack! I say! Augusta, come here! Maybe you'll be able to understand a little better! Is this the same old hag who... fattens the children?"

He was comic tragic inside his loose, light blue strip flannel pyjamas, trying to understand in the dead of night what this new pratfall was all about. They stayed up almost all night. Lela was giving and the other two were receiving promises that she would never ever do anything for anybody again, especially Josephina, especially anything suggested by Old Voula. She was weeping inconsolably, wiping her eyes with her shawl so that they turned even redder. She also took out a small tissue from up her sleeve and blew her nose. Every now and then she'd jerk from the sobs. At some point, she asked permission to go to her room. Augusta started telling

Mario about Lela's dangerous interests and her even more dangerous initiatives. Mario, however, cut her short.

"*Indeed, but when she took the child to the old woman and she spread honey on her, do you remember that you forbade me to talk to her? You said that I was too abrupt and that I would hurt her feelings! You took on the responsibility of bringing her to her senses! So don't you tell me about Lela's initiatives! Tomorrow morning we'll have an even stricter talk! If she doesn't conform, then your mother can have her since you all care about her so much! I won't have her here! And you know what they say back in my village... that even he holy man needs to be frightened from time to time!*"

The next day, they went over all the *prohibitions* and the *don'ts*. Lela agreed. She also apologized. Many times. As far as the mumps was concerned, it finally cleared up without the help of the tar...

Chapter 12   Aristides and Maria.

THE OLD Levy was a small, perfectly square and high ceilinged, one storey building. It was said that once upon a time, the Turk who collected tax from all those who entered the city, whatever they were, visitors, passersby or permanent residents, lived there. It had a wooden door and two tiny windows on opposite sides. For many years it had been left deserted until it became the home to two homeless siblings with empty stomachs and twisted minds, according to the people who lived around there. Augusta, however, was one of those who believed that simply the circumstances of life, whatever they were, were to blame for the situation they were in and added that not only was their mind not twisted... but they had a lot of intelligence which they simply hadn't learnt how to manage correctly. Aristides and Maria. Two weird and pitiable figures... Two human beings with tormented souls. Two poor devils. Two vagabonds of the times.

ARISTIDES was funny and quainter than Maria. Spry and well fed like a tom cat; of medium height and built with a stout, but not overweight. A round, plump face like a full moon, with light blue, cunningly dumb eyes and a permanent smile on his similarly cunningly dumb looking face. He had a blond, wild mustache which looked like a Turk's head and blondish hair which was tinged with grey. With a cloth cap permanently on his head which he only took off briefly to scratch and then quickly put back it on again. With a nicely shaped nose and two protruding ears which were big and round. With a hint of a beard and the same wardrobe for years; a very long ankle lengths probably cream, smock made of canvas fabric, with long sleeves and only two or three buttons while the rest of the button holes gaped empty, and a belt of the same fabric, hanging to one side. It was said to have been a present from some butcher who had changed professions and had given the smock to Aristides, and from that time on, the older people never saw him again without it. His favourite accessory was his crook. As for shoes? He hated them! He had some but never wore them. His favourite habit was to lie on the floor from time to time, with his head turned towards the door and to peep through the crack with his crook in hand. With the curved end of his crook, he'd grab the calf of any woman who happened to go by. The woman would scream, Aristides would laugh. The woman would threaten to call the gendarme, Aristides would laugh even harder, because that was what they all said but none had ever called any gendarme.

MARIA looked exactly like the *"Mad Woman"* of *Théodore Géricault*[33]. The two women had the same way of looking and unlike Aristides, she never smiled.

She was tight-lipped, always solemn and expressionless but always polite. Her dried tissues, as thin as membrane, stubbornly covered the bones of her face. She had dark eyes, was shorter than her brother, very skinny, and walked in a quick and bowed manner. She always wore a head scarf sometimes a grayish and sometimes a brownish one, thick socks all year round and always a skirt which was far too big for her. Even though it was a narrow line skirt, she cut it to size with safety pins that could often be seen. She'd pin them all around the waist and they'd form even numbered pleats.

---

[33] *Oil painting* by the French pioneer of the *Romantic Movement, Théodore Gericault (1823). Musée des Beaux Arts de Lyon,* France.

Chapter 12   Aristides and Maria.

And of course, Maria wore shoes. They might not have always been her size, but she did at least wear them. Maria's mascot for many years had been a rooster. She would take it with her wherever she went. She would hold it in her arms tightly and protectively, with the same tenderness that others held their child. On other occasions it would hop beside her in order to catch up with her since she always double marched.

She washed their scant clothes, whatever they were, in an open spout which spilled its water near the last houses of the town and into the river. She'd hang them on the bushes and the tussocks to dry; sometimes when Maria returned to collect her dry laundry she burst into tears on seeing that the sudden breeze had already blown it away. Then the women with the multicolored rose patterned headscarves, threw aside their pickaxes and spades and set to immediately to collect together Maria's laundry. Most times they chased after the flying laundry and they screamed in laughter as they ran after it and stumbled here and there on the ground, between the recently-dug furrows. And when, finally, they put their freshly washed clothes into her lap, they offered her the hem of their skirts to wipe the tears from her eyes until she was smiling.

THE WOMEN with the multicolored rose patterned headscarves, their long skirts and their wide, short white galoshes, had come from far off Caucasus. They made their living by tilling the land, planting vegetable seeds and caring for all the young plants from daybreak to night fall, in the large field alongside the river which wended its way towards the sea and which, despite being full of water all year round, people used to call it *Dried River*. Later, they sold their produce at the local Saturday market up on the main road.

Maria, a woman of few words, who was talkative in their company only, had made friends of these women. And when Maria washed her hair, they plaited it; sometimes in one plait, at other times in two.

Sometimes she agreed to sit with and eat with them during the short break they had at lunchtime. Then they used to sing any song from their far away country in a language which to Maria was unknown but she smiled as well as nodded her head back and forth attempting to find the rhythm of the song. But, anytime one of the women looked at her, then Maria immediately stopped both smiling and nodding her head, and looked down at her feet or the ground like a child ashamed and embarrassed. As far as the songs are concerned, they're the same ones which are heard on the air every day, with the sounds of the nature, by requests made out loud by all those who worked in the neighbouring fields from the other bank of the riverbed with the noise the ploughs made as they dug the earth, and reaching as far as from the one side of the river to the other.

And whenever Aristides went there, he stood on his side, and placed his crook in the ground; he leant with his two hands on the top of his crook, rested his cheek on them and tried to be their audience. It was obvious that poor Aristides didn't want to interrupt or destroy these moments but as soon as Maria noticed that he was there, she jumped up and hurriedly thanked the women with the multicolored rose patterned head scarves; she removed the apron she used to wear over her skirt, put in it her clean laundry, and holding the folded apron carefully, she left, despite Aristides objections. He inevitable looked worried, feeling that he was the cause of interrupting that spirited music time.

Chapter 12   Aristides and Maria.

No one could tell for certain who these two were and where they had come from, whether if they had always been like that or if something had happened and made them that way. It was heard, without being certified, that they had a brother, a military doctor who had been killed in the war, somewhere in Albania; that they had been born rich but for some reason had lost everything, that the government had granted them the Levy to live in, as it had been unused for years... Quite aside the fact that the government seemed to acknowledge daily their deceased brother's tribute, in this way...

Be that as it may, without them ever extending a hand to beg, it was the locals who supported them, giving them a bit of food, a bit of money, or some clothes, even though sometimes these were even more pathetic than those two, that's why when Maria saw that the cast-offs she was given were actually for the trash, she'd refuse to take them, saying *"We have enough, we have enough!"* without further ado.

Daily, at around noon, she returned from the baker's with a freshly baked loaf of bread under her arm. These were the only moments when she was truly happy and looked content and blissful in the way she'd hold the daily, freshly baked, warm bread with an air of assurance under her arm...

They never created any problems to the neighborhood or the town, apart from Aristides' hobby and his passion for women's calves! Moreover, the mothers of the neighborhood never scared their children by pointing to Aristides.
Everybody liked them and everybody cared about them even if some of them showed it only once or twice times a year, like at Christmas for example... Plenty were those who, on leaving Meltos' bakery, would stop outside the Levy, give a holler, and

one of the siblings would come out and be given a bit of the freshly cooked food, whatever it might have been.

THEN CAME the time they had all awaited but hardly anyone wished for, at least not as long as Aristides and Maria lived... because all the neighbors liked Aristides and Maria and they would overlook even Aristides capers. So the time had come for the new road to replace the old road which passed in front of the Levy. It was going to be a wide avenue with flowers and high street lights on the safety zone which would split the road in half. The houses on the left and right of the street were going to relinquish a section of their front yards in order to help in the accomplishment of the project. It was the road they had been waiting for which would improve the neighborhood's image; raise the value of their property and change their daily routine for the better for a thousand reasons.

But... then the whole neighborhood remembered Aristides and Maria... They remembered them when they were informed that the old Levy had to be demolished first, so that work on the new road construction could begin, since according to the engineers' plans, the old Levy stood right in the middle of the wide avenue. At that point, for the first time the neighbors felt what they had never felt till then for Aristides and Maria, and which it had never crossed their minds that they would feel. They were filled with boundless sorrow at the mere thought that two beings were going to be thrown on the streets since the only thing which seemed to belong to them was that old Levy; a small room less than four by four which happened to be their home. It was the only thing they had. The old Levy and their poverty. Nothing else.

Chapter 12   Aristides and Maria.

Suddenly, even those who had never shown any sympathy towards the two indigents of their neighborhood or those who, in general, had no such heart-strings to be tugged, found themselves fighting against the construction of the road. They did everything they could to suspend the project until a solution could be found for the two homeless people. They began by announcing the problem to the whole city. Residents from other areas would come to Aristides and Maria's neighborhood daily. The authorities responsible began to search for a solution which would be in the best interests of Aristides and Maria. In the meantime, the residents placed their cars along the whole length of the old road and didn't move them for many a day. Everyone pushed as hard as they could. Names and signatures kept on being added to the petition of support that Galatia had thought up, after her talk with her lawyer husband. When it got filled up, Joan the Americana brought another one. Thousands took part in that sympathetic protest outside Aristides and Maria's old Levy, which lasted from spring until halfway through autumn.

Shortly before the first rains started, a solution was found. The two siblings were to be housed on the ground floor of a three-storey mansion by a previous Mayor of the town.
He had been living somewhere in Europe for the last couple of years and he had been informed about the dilemma by his caretaker who had been looking after and maintaining the mansion of the former first man of town.
To be more precise, this was not to be a temporarily solution... but for as long as they wanted, for as long as they lived... And that's how it happened.

WHOEVER later met Aristides, first and foremost realized that he was wearing shoes! Moreover, that he was dressed like a gentleman and that he wasn't holding a crook anymore, but a pocket watch which he would constantly take out of his pocket, look at, try to see what time it was and laugh. Instead of wearing a cloth cap he now wore an authentic panama hat which he still tended to take off, as he had done back then with his cloth cap, scratch his head and put back on again.

Poor Maria wore a skirt as always but which was now new and her size, and brand new low heels. Her greyish hair wasn't covered with a hair scarf anymore. When she was seen on the street, it was always the same time, around noon. She would be holding a freshly baked, warm loaf of bread under her arm and in the other had a shopping bag which she had in order to transport her rooster with her, and she still walked with that same well known stride of hers, as if she were marching. She was still polite and taciturn. She replied in the same way to everybody when asked.

"We're fine! God bless you all, thank you very much!" and she would then disappear in a hurry.

THE PLANS for the wide avenue were modified a bit after the intervention of the old Mayor, who knew how to pull strings better than his successors. Aristides and Maria may not have been in need of a home now but the neighbors, who had come to love them and some -who were growing up with or had already grown up with them in the same neighborhood- insisted that the old Levy had to remain where it was in their honor. All around Aristides and Maria's old Levy, which wasn't moved an inch, a beautiful, iron pavilion was built, with elaborate designs and a round roof which looked like an

Chapter 12   Aristides and Maria.

open umbrella. The calligraphic initials A and M at the top of the wind-vane reminded everyone who had ever met them, liked them, loved them and helped them, who gave but also received from them without their knowing, of Aristides and Maria. Very often, people who have never met them dwell for a while, with their gaze following the letters turning in the stirring of the wind, and ask what they stand for. There is always somebody passing by to tell them a few words about the poor siblings, who in their later lives were helped by fate and the love of people more than they had ever been helped before... So, Aristides' and Maria's story is learnt by those who never had the fortune of meeting them...

LILY TSONI

Whoever knows anything about the following persons are, kindly requested to contact the placement services for persons through the Greek Red Cross... We are seeking Parthena or Pepi ...tzoglou, born in Smyrna of Asia Minor on December 25th 1922, 40 years of age today. She has blond, curly hair, blue eyes and a big birth mark in the shape of a chestnut on her left shoulder. Her mother, Gesthimani, was a teacher in an all girls' school and her father, Mikes, a doctor by occupation. On the 25th November 1925, the ...tzoglou family, departed on a ship from the port of Smyrna for Thessaloniki.

At the port of Thessaloniki, on... November 1925, due to the crowding and congestion, the then three year old, then, Parthena or Pepi, disappeared. On the day of her disappearance she was wearing a blue, woolen dress with white checks, a red knit coatee with two pompons around the neckline, black boots and white socks. Her hair was plaited in two braids and she was holding a cloth doll with a porcelain face in her arms, Aisha. Parthena or Pepi ...tzoglou is being sought by her siblings, Stratigoula, Eudoksia and Nikolaos. Whoever knows anything about Parthena or Pepi ...tzoglou, is kindly requested to contact..."

Every afternoon, Lela would sit with her ear glued to the radio, at the time of the announcement of the G.R.C. bulletin, which tried to find missing persons from Asia Minor. Lela also did the same thing in order to listen to which ships left from the port of Piraeus and to which islands they went. She had learnt by heart the names of each ship liner, just as she had learnt by heart the correct sequence of the harbors they'd each stop at... "*Camellia*", time 4:00 to Syros, Tinos, Mykonos... Santorini[34].

---

[34] *Syros, Tinos, Myconos, Santorini:* Four of the many, beautiful, *white* Greek islands in the Aegeon Pelagos (Aegean Sea).

Chapter 13   Placement services for persons
               through the Greek Red Cross.

"Chania", time 5:00 to Iraklion[35]... She'd listen to the navigation bulletin and she knew for which ships departure was forbidden due to high seas.

DURING the last three days, she'd listened more carefully and meticulously to the bulletin of Placement for Persons through the Greek Red Cross. She'd listen and hold her breath. She'd listen and keep notes in her notepad. The one she wrote the day's shopping in so that she wouldn't forget what she had to buy.

And maybe her ear may not have caught all the details correctly, but she was almost positive that Parthena, who was being sought by her siblings, was none other than that beautiful lady Mrs. Kakia, the doctor with the long, blond hair, the blue eyes and the brown birthmark on her left shoulder. She was sure that she had seen that birthmark on the doctor's shoulder but she couldn't remember when. Neither could she remember whether it looked like a chestnut. She could swear on the bible that Mrs. Kakia's was chestnut shaped, but it existed and she was sure of that. Then again, Lela couldn't remember if it was on her left shoulder or on her right, but what difference did it make? It was still on shoulder!

Furthermore, everyone in town knew that Mrs. Kakia wasn't brought up by the parents who had given birth to her. It was said that Mr. Thalis, her father, who was also a doctor, just like the missing Parthena or Pepi's father, had happened to be in Thessaloniki once and found, without anyone ever knowing all

---

[35] *Iraklion*: The capital city of the Greek island of *Creta*.

the details, a little forsaken girl whom he had brought home with him. He kept her and adopted her. He raised her together with his wife and made her their daughter. Of course the vindictive gossips said that the doctor had supposedly had her with another woman and that he acknowledged her when he finally saw that his legal wife, Marika, would never bear children. But Lela couldn't care less about what they said...

Kakia the doctoress, as she was referred to by most people, Lela one of them, was now married to a professor. She had two children and she had become a pathologist, like her father, and still had black hair and blue eyes. If only she had the birthmark on her shoulder too...

Lela met her in her surgery. She waited patiently for her turn in the waiting room. She was fifth in line when she arrived. Another three showed up after her and she gave up her turn to them without them asking for it. She had to be the last one. The last. She had to be alone when she spoke to the doctor. She shouldn't be pressed for time when she began slowly dishing out her thoughts and assumptions. Let alone that she didn't know where to begin and how to end with her deed of daring. She had told Augusta that she had had a stomachache all night.

"Here, right here! It kept me awake all night. I am not in pain now but I think I'll go to the doctor around noon." Lela lied as she was afraid that she would be in trouble if she revealed exactly what she had in mind. The truth was that Lela had indeed stayed up all night, not because of the pain though. She had no pain but her mind dwelt on the missing Parthena or Pepi who could be Mrs. Kakia, Kakia the doctoress. She found the idea of the lost siblings all meeting

Chapter 13   Placement services for persons
              through the Greek Red Cross.

up again very thrilling and it would not only be thanks to the G.R.C. but also to herself. She shivered all night with emotion and she cried as well. However, what if it wasn't like that? What if the doctor got angry and told her off on top of that? No, No! Lela would dare, even if she were wrong. It was worth trying.

It was exactly one thirty in the afternoon when the last patient came out of the consulting room. Lela stood up with a heart that was kicking wildly in her chest, virtually breaking it. Kakia was standing in the doorway, beckoning her to go in. She was pretty in her white robe. She was a beautiful doctor. She asked Lela about Augusta and Josephina.

"I will see Mario later today. I brought some nice wool from Scotland and I want to talk to him about what to tailor for me" she said but Lela didn't even hear her. The only thing she could hear was the beating of her heart which continued to kick mercilessly in her chest. The only thing she wanted to do was to run away before she became embroiled in something she'd regret. *"I have to go before I make a fool of myself"*, she thought. The doctor diagnosed her fear and anxiety and held her by the shoulders.

"Lela, Lela? What's wrong? You've turned pale! Is that how awful you feel, then? Come, tell me everything! Come now, Lela! What's the matter?"

Lela started crying. When the going got rough, she always cried. The doctor stroked her hair.

"Don't be afraid! Whatever it is! Come on, tell me! And first of all, does Augusta know you are here? Ah, she knows!

Great! Then, you haven't come in secrecy! Or maybe Augusta doesn't know why you're here exactly? Are we hiding something from her? We can if we have to! Let's talk about it first!" She succeeded in winning her trust.

Lela started shyly.

"I came... came, not for me! I mean, it's my decision to come but I have come for you! Not for me! For you! Yes indeed, to... I'll tell you, I'll tell you everything! But please, don't interrupt me! If you interrupt, I'll stop and leave! Now that I can say it all, can start... just let me!"

Kakia leaned against the examination bed, crossed her arms on her chest and committed herself to listening while Lela continued to talk breathlessly.

"I, you see... I listen to the bulletin of the Red Cross because I like it! I get sad when I hear that people have gone missing and have lost their families, but I like it! I cry for the children that have been lost by their mothers, but I want to listen to it all!! I remember all the announcements by heart! And when after a while I don't hear one of them anymore, I am happy! I say, there!... they have found him or they have found her! Even if it's not the case! Even if the people just got bored and ceased to make the announcement. I want to believe that this is not the case, but that they have found their person... or they have found their child. Yesterday and the day before I didn't get a wink of sleep all night! Especially last night! I was disturbed by the bulletin of the Red Cross! I mean, not all of it! It was new! A new announcement! I didn't sleep till morning! All night I was trying to decide what to do today! To come or not to come! Oh, wait a second, so I don't forget!

Chapter 13   Placement services for persons through the Greek Red Cross.

It's the most important thing of all! Can I first see the shoulder with the birthmark? It's the left, isn't it? The left is the one with the birthmark, right? Please, don't ask! Now that I've started, don't stop me! Let me see it! Just for a second!" Now that her cowardice had gone for a walk, Lela was talking non-stop.

The doctor uncrossed her arms, took her stethoscope off her neck and placed it on the metal table with the wheels, next to her. She was dazed but she pulled her robe down a little bit over her left shoulder after she had unbuttoned several buttons. She also pulled aside the white shirt she was wearing underneath and her shoulder was revealed. The left. As much as was needed in order to reveal her brown birthmark. Like a big blotch in the shape of a chestnut. Yes, it looked like a chestnut. Lela started rejoicing.

"Oh, my! It is like a chestnut! Like a real small chestnut! So, you still have it! You have it! And since when have you had it, Mrs. Kakia? Since when?"

"Since when have I had it? The birthmark? Since...forever... I don't know! Ever since I remember myself! Maybe from the day I was born! Lela started up with this birthmark on my shoulder! Lela, for heaven's sake, what is going on with you? I'm sure you didn't come all this way to talk about my birthmark! And, I'm even more certain you didn't stay up all night because of it! So, tell me! Talk!"

"I did come for your birthmark! And for you! And for your blue eyes and your blond hair! And you must be now around forty years old, aren't you?"

"OK! I am around that! So, what? How would it help if you knew my age?"

"I'll tell you why... On the bulletin of the Red Cross, the people are looking for a Parthena. They are trying to find a Parthena with blue eyes and black hair. I mean, Parthena is her name. That's how she was baptized. And she has a brown birthmark on her left shoulder. A birthmark in the shape of a chestnut, they said. And she is of your age. And I have heard that you have been adopted! And that Mrs. Marika, your mother, didn't give birth to you! It is said that your father may have had you with another woman and that Mrs. Marika accepted you but I don't really believe this story! Your father is not that sort of man! However, everyone knows that these people here are not your parents! So, I thought that maybe you should look for Parthena's siblings who are looking for her too, because I am certain, in fact I bet my life on it, that you Mrs. Kakia are Parthena! Now you can swear at me, scold me, tell me off, do whatever you want! You'd be right, whatever you say to me! However, I didn't come here to make you go out of your mind, nor play with your feelings! I came because I can't get out of my mind, not for a minute, that you are indeed Parthena!" She let out a comic sigh, deflating with relief.

Kakia was left with her mouth gaping wide open with her eyes like saucers. She got up and went straight to the mirror. There was a mirror on the wall beside the examination bed. She touched her hair and untied the lacing that kept it pulled back. She held her hair with one hand and brought it forward towards her right cheek. She stuck her nose up against the mirror. She looked at her hair as if she was seeing what color it was for the first time. It was blond.

"It's blond!" she mumbled.

Chapter 13 Placement services for persons through the Greek Red Cross.

Then she tossed her hair to the back. She leaned forward again, as close as she could to the mirror. She looked at her eyes. They were blue.

"They're blue!" she confirmed, as if she were seeing them also for the first time.

She pulled the sleeve of the white robe down again. She did the same with the white shirt underneath. She allowed the birthmark on her shoulder to reveal itself again. She looked at it for quite a while, in the mirror. It really looked like an average, nicely shaped chestnut, lying on her shoulder.

"My God, my little chestnut!" she whispered, as though she had suddenly remembered its existence.

"And they called her "Pepi" when she was young, that was before they lost her! I'm talking about her, Parthena! They called her "Pepi", yes!" Lela started up as she saw that she wasn't in any immediate danger, as the doctor wasn't mad at all. At least not yet.

"Pepi? You said... "Pepi?" The surprise was now obvious at every single thing that she heard coming out of Lela's mouth which had to do with the missing Parthena! *"But... there is always in my mind, deep inside it, a little voice, yes, it is a child's voice, calling out "Pepi! Pepi! Come out and play!" Years now! As far back as I can remember, I hear this little voice calling out! And always in my sleep! That's why I've never paid any attention! Yes, now I'm sure that it was calling me! As... as for my parents, yes... well, yes! They told me the day of my graduation that I wasn't their child. They didn't give birth to me, they said but they adored me. They had kept*

it a secret, they said, because they didn't know how I was going to take it. They were afraid that I'd leave as soon as I found out that I wasn't theirs. Many children do that. They had kept it a secret until I had got all the provisions I needed to ensure a good job. They were afraid that I'd drop everything, them and my education. "Now, we can tell you! Whatever decisions you may make, even if you decide to leave us!" they had said. Of course, I didn't desert them. How could I? They were my parents for me, I didn't know I had others who had given birth to me though!
My father said he had found me at the port of Thessaloniki amongst the vast concourse of refugees. I was a well dressed child although a bit dirty from the voyage and the tears. I was crying when he found me. Crying for my mother and I wanted to eat. I was hungry. I was certainly a little refugee. Lost. Rootless. He had searched together with a policeman. A man of the port authorities helped them try to find my family. But to no avail. It was bloody chaos! Ships kept on arriving, continuously! The fugitives in droves. They believed in the end that I could have been -and why not- an orphan! My father kept me. Oh God! Lela, tell me exactly what you've heard! And what time the next bulletin of the Red Cross is? Can I make it?"

Now it was Lela's turn for her jaw to drop and her eyes to open wide. Mumbling and deeply moved she tried to continue.

"You mean... so it's true? Parthena is you, Mrs. Kakia? You are from Asia Minor? A Smyrnian, I mean? Here... I've written it all down here! Look, her mother's name is Gesthimani and her father's Mikes. It said that the little girl

Chapter 13   Placement services for persons
              through the Greek Red Cross.

was wearing a check dress! Blue and white! I couldn't catch the rest, the dates and the last name... She was holding a doll in her arms! I didn't get the name because the woman who announces the bulletin of the Red Cross..., I'm not saying, she doesn't speak clearly, but a bit too fast for me!"

Lela, returned home merry as a grig and as jolly as a fiddle. She told Augusta everything in chapter and verse.

"However, the exact opposite could have happened, Kakia could have got angry and you could have been in really hot water. Next time, inform me. Good for you, though! You did well! At least up to this point! The rest is Kakia's business" Augusta had said.

THE DOCTORESS Kakia, listened to the bulletin of the Greek Red Cross together with the whole family. That same evening at around four. Together with her children and her husband. Together with her two parents. Those who hadn't given birth to her but who had adored her. Those who hadn't given life to her but who had filled her life with all the love they had inside their hearts. Firstly Kakia had talked it over with them. She asked if they agreed on her next steps or if they had objections.

"I'll do whatever you tell me to! You know how much I love you!" she had reassured them. They agreed with any hesitation that she had to find her roots, the family that bore her.

A short while before the program, Kakia's mother, Mrs. Marika, had taken out of the old kist, the blue dress with the white checks that the little fugitive was wearing back then at the port of Thessaloniki, where Mr. Thalis had found her wondering around in tears. And the red knit coatee with the two pompons, a pair of white, cotton bobby-socks and her black shoes that looked like boots. And a worn cloth doll with brown hair that was painted on her little porcelain head which she held tightly in her arms to get her to sleep, right up to the end of primary school, and now she understood why...The doll who she always called Aisa. With hands and voice that were shaky, that wonderful lady, Mrs. Marika, gave them to Kakia.

"Hold them! I've kept them for this moment so that you and your parents could be sure one day of your identity. Look at them carefully, during the whole time the announcement is being made. So that we can grasp whether it's true. If it really is about you".

Everybody's eyes were moist with tears. Kakia was tearful and nervous. She was listening but shaking at the same time. Mrs. Marika was holding her by the shoulders, standing behind her. Her legs couldn't hold her any longer though, so she also sat down next to her on the couch.

Everything tied in with the day that Mr. Thalis found her, with the day that little Parthena or Pepi had got lost at the port of Thessaloniki. An hour before he'd found her, the ship with the refugees had arrived. The clothes, the doll that she was holding, everything was the same.

"Dear, God! Do you think, do you think I am she? Do you think that's me? Do you?" Kakia kept asking, wracked with emotion.

They called right away. Everything was settled. She met up with the family, through the Red Cross's bulletin of placement for persons, the very next day in Athens.

Chapter 13   Placement services for persons
              through the Greek Red Cross.

IT WAS SHE. Kakia was no other than the missing Parthena or Pepi! They had searched for her; they said they searched for a long time. For years. Nobody had been able to give them any clue as to how to find their little girl. Her father had died from the heartache of losing his child. For years and years he kept the doctors of Thessaloniki on the lookout for some little girl and later on for a woman of his daughter's age with blond hair and blue eyes and a brownish birthmark on the left shoulder. No one though had ever examined such a girl. Nor an adolescent. Nor a woman later on.
"If only he had made that same move on a national level..." Kakia was thinking.

Her mother was alive. Very old though, with senile dementia most of the time. They placed the dress, that Kakia was wearing when they found her, in her hands.

"This is Parthena's! Why isn't Parthena wearing it? I made it myself with the help of Aisha!" She said, thumping her black cane on the floor. *"She isn't wearing her coatee either? Pepi, where are you? Get dressed! You'll catch a cold!"* and she banged her black walking stick with the silver handle on the floor. Kakia wrapped her arms around her mother, crying.

They all had tears in their eyes. Kakia nested in her arms, in tears.

Stratigoula, since she was the oldest, confirmed and clarified that indeed that dress definitely belonged to Parthena. Without a doubt. Their mother had sewn it with the help of the Turkish neighbour who helped them with the house chores. Her name was Aisha. Little Pepi loved the Turkish woman so much that she had named her doll after her. She understood then why she had called her doll Aisha for so many years and refused to give her any other name when they asked her what sort of name that was and how it had come to her.

And the red coatee, their mother had knitted it and the other two sisters had an identical one.

In addition, apart from the birthmark on the shoulder, which was Parthena's personal trademark and which her brother used to call her 'little chestnut' because of its shape, she looked tremendously like her sister. They could even have been twins, but indeed were not, since Kakia was three years younger than her.

Everyone was happy at the reunion taking place. Mr. Thalis confessed to Kakia that he was now finally relieved because for so many years he had lived with the guilt that he had deprived a child of its family, albeit involuntarily, " *but believe me... I couldn't leave you unprotected in a lake, amongst the walnuts of every walnut tree, just a child... at least now I know that I have done no wrong. The only thing I can't understand is how those two people, the policeman and the coast guard, did not hear your family was looking for you. It is strange, unless they simply didn't care...*"

Mrs. Marika and Mr. Thalis, certain that Kakia would agree and would really wish it so, asked for and took with them the old mother who lived with her lost daughter's name. Kakia displayed, in the best place in her surgery and in her home, two pictures that had been taken in Smyrna a short while before she had taken the road of refugees with her family. In one of them, she was wearing the same blue, white checked

Chapter 13   Placement services for persons
through the Greek Red Cross.

dress. Another authentic sign of the past. In the other, she was in her father's arms in his surgery in Smyrna.

After some time, she asked Lela to tell her how she had known about her birthmark, about her *little chestnut* as she herself called it.

"You see, I have never shown it to anyone. As a child and as a teen I was embarrassed by it. Later on, I didn't want it to be seen even at the beach. Apart from my parents and my husband, no one else has ever seen it!" she explained.

"Oh, really? And I thought that I had seen it! I had heard of this birthmark though! I am sure! I was waiting outside the screen at Mr. Mario's shop and you were having a fitting and told him to be careful not to prick the birthmark on your shoulder with a pin because it's a dangerous thing! Gee, how the mind plays tricks! And I thought I had really seen it! But, why do you care even if I had seen it? You have profited from that birthmark! From the birthmark and people's gossip! Because if I hadn't heard the gossip, that Mrs. Marika hadn't given birth to you and the rest of the story and if I hadn't heard you talking about a birthmark on your shoulder, I doubt very much that you would have found your family! Because there are many Parthenas and Pepis! Even blue-eyed women with blond hair! Them being adopted though and them having a birthmark on the left shoulder and in the shape of a chestnut at that, well, I don't think there could be more than one!"

LILY TSONI

THE CHILDREN of the neighborhood would stop their chasing until *he* passed by and then continue their game as soon as he descended the narrow footpath which had been curved out through the years between a stone-built dwarf wall and the fence that penned the big alley, with the useless old trucks and cars which lay in there, most of them without tires; windows broken; upholstery ripped; and missing their seats, with bare steering wheels and broken gear shifts and with a lot of rust both inside and out. Inside this car cemetery, the children pretended to be drivers but rarely passengers. Each one who took the place of the driver usually did the driving standing up as there were no seats. They were heard making the sound of the car's engine. Their hands turned the steering wheel and changed gears. "Broom-Broom! Giang! Giang, giaaang!" Naturally, the children also replicated the horn with their mouths too. "Beep-beep! Beeeep!"

Each young driver reliquished his turn to the next who waited patiently in line, when he got bored or was called home by his mother. The children who happened to be the drivers or to be exact, the drivers and the car when *he* passed, would stop at once until *he* left.

HE HAD SPRUNG up like a mushroom in autumn. He was very tall, rather skinny, with blond hair, almost certainly cropped short, at least from what could be seen from his forehead and temples through that black knit cloth cap which he didn't seem to take off his head all year round. He didn't take it off the following summer, or the summer after that either. His face had the reddish complexion of the northern and eastern peoples of Europe. His eyes were blue and bright. He looked tanned and probably was but his rosy complexion

Chapter 14 Our very own spy.

looked soft and smooth and the few wrinkles he had must have been expression lines. His broad smile originated from his shapely but rather small mouth, and spread across the whole of his face. A smile that took quite some time to grace the children of the neighborhood, as he passed in front of them and they stared at him strangely and inquisitively. Most of them with their mouths gaping wide open. And whenever they returned the smile, it was coincidental, shy and awkward, and then they'd continue the game they had stopped for his sake.

He always wore the same short, firmly tied, dark boots -which could have been army boots- over his dark trousers. His similarly dark overcoat was a type of short ulster and was always buttoned up; its belt always fastened in its silver buckle. He carried a small bundle on his back daily, a cloth saddle bag like an overstuffed, medium sized pillow, something between a sack and a bag which hung at the end of a stick just like the passers-by in fairytales, and he held the other end in front of his chest with his right hand.

He had a very characteristic walk, a weird, disjointed and clumsy walk. He seemed to be trying however, to find a better stride. His stride wasn't fast or slow but he always looked hasty. It may have been his legs which were very long and the way in which they spread apart while he walked, which left a great distance between them. No one from the neighbourhood ever found out from where he had come or where he was going. Then again, no one ever tried to find out even though they were all dying of curiosity.

He'd pass by every afternoon, always at the same time. Shortly before dusk. He was rarely late and when he was, he'd pass by a little while before vespers or a little after.

He was a man from nowhere who was, however, going somewhere. An endless coming and going which lasted almost three years. In the beginning they all called him *the old man*. Later, rumors had it that he was a spy. Some wanted him to be Bulgarian. Most of them. Others wanted him to be Russian. They said that he wore a mask. He looked sixty to sixty-five years old. Others made him seventy. Those, however, who had the chance to see him up close, and combining that with his voice which was very high pitched and very youthful, were sure that he wore a mask which disfigured him in an attempt to look much older than his age.

NOT forgetting Vizier-Georgena who claimed to see him every day. She was the shepherd who took her ship out to pasture usually with her husband, Vizier-George. He was ageless and used to stand, almost stone-still, leaning with his two arms on his crook, while whenever necessary it was his wife who ran after the sheep. So, Vizier-Georgena said that close to where the sheep grazed, in the olive groves beside the big road which descended from the north and lead to the villages of the south, a big, black car stopped every evening.

"It is long and sleek like a government vehicle!" she said. She didn't, of course explain what she meant by *government vehicle* but her husband and their helper confirmed what she said.

Her husband also took it a step further and boldly stated that somewhere on that ridge among the old olive groves, the *spy* would sometimes talk on the wireless transmission -he'd take or give orders and information, or something like that- at

Chapter 14   Our very own spy.

times he'd talk for a while with the men in the car and at other times he'd do both.

"Indeed, that's the way it is!" Vizier-Georgena confirmed, adding that she had seen him not only *"pressing some buttons"* but also *"putting something in his ears and on his head"*, like the hair band her daughters wore on their head. Finally, they said that they saw him eating the food which had been brought in the car, sitting on that ridge. The only objection the woman had, had to do with the W/T[36]. She claimed that he carried it inside that saddle bag he had over his shoulder while their helper insisted that someone from inside the car gave it to him and he then took it away when they left. Her husband agreed with her. He said that sometimes the car was a little late and the *spy* occupied himself with it while waiting or sometimes he'd wait for the car to leave and then he'd talk on the W/T.

"Don't say a word to anyone though..." Vizier-Georgena would say, *"cause they'll shut us all up in jail!"*

So after the *old man* who had become a *spy*, finished his business, whatever that may have been, he returned along the same road well after dusk. The children of the neighborhood continued to play. They stopped again until he'd passed by. Then, they'd immerse themselves in their game again until their mothers called them home.

As time passed by, he smiled on them. Occasionally, without stopping, he spoke to them in his low voice. Sometimes he'd talk to them with that high pitched voice of his *"How are you?" "Have you been a good boy today?"*

---
[36] *Wireless Transmission.*

The children would then run into their yards, shouting at the top of their lungs to the grownups: *"The old man talked to me! He asked me how I was!" "The spy asked me if I was a good boy and I said yes!"* And they'd immerse themselves in their game again until their mothers called them for bed.

It was still a mystery as to where he'd spend his night. Maybe the people from another neighborhood knew the answer; perhaps they in turn didn't know where he went and what he did every evening. And out of the whole of their neighborhood, Lela believed that it was she who knew the most...

MARION and Abigail, Joan's the Americana's sisters, were playing tennis on Georgis' tennis court one evening; a piece of land in the garden which he had turned into a court.
Abigail, who was a painter, believed that the spy was an intriguing subject.

Either way, the subjects she worked on were anthropocentric. She flung her tennis racket down and climbed the stairs two by two to get her camera. Joan explained to her the reason why she needn't hurry.
Her topic was an everyday stroll through the neighbourhood, at the same time without fail.

In the days that came, Abigail would put up her easel, sometimes on the patio and at others times in the garden, doing a series of portraits of *our very own spy,* as she called him.

Chapter 14   Our very own spy.

Before that though, she had to stretch her hand out in front of her, measuring with her pencils the distances she wanted, trying very hard not to be noticed by her *subject*. It was quite easy for her. First of all, when the spy got outside the house, he'd turn his head in search of the pretty American, looking at her straight in the eye.

What's more, he can't have known a lot about painting. He'd see her appear, running two to three steps in front of him; sideways across from him; holding her pencil in her outstretched arm; right in front of him since the only thing that separated them was the fence, and he'd show his enjoyment by smiling so much broadly like an impressionable child, he can't find the right words to express it and he simply can only smile.

She'd run with swift choppy steps opposite him and even though she still focused on his face, she'd walk backwards, trying to get the measurements she needed for his cheekbones and eyes, his chin and forehead, his ears and nose.

She tried to get the axis she needed to work on his face and she succeeded in doing so, a bit at a time, and he didn't even notice. It was obvious that he was looking at her, enjoying her innocent, girlish and simultaneously doll-like face, as he saw a child in it, cutting capers and playing.

He might have wished *"I hope I see her tomorrow"* because surely she made his day even though he was always left with the unanswered question *"Has she gone mad?"* Not of course that the neighbors ever understood any better than the spy what in the world she was doing, running up and down behind the fence every time she saw him...

As suddenly as he had arrived, just as suddenly he had stopped coming.

It wasn't only that the hour of dusk had lost the mysterious charm lent to it by the enigmatic foreigner; the old man with the youthful voice; the Russian or the Bulgarian spy... there was no difference... It was that he was terribly missed by everyone. By the children; by the mothers. The latter, because they no longer had anyone to use to scare their children with! Up until then, they had had him..."Behave, or else I'll give you to the spy!"

Chapter 15   A green-bottle with a stitch.

IT WAS A LITTLE bug; chubby, fluffy and golden-green. It was also shiny, not bigger then a medium sized almond. Its body was hard, it was something like a shuck. You didn't have time to count how many legs it had as they were constantly moving, they gathered and spread in a strange way incessantly.

Stathis, Sotiria's brother, had caught it. They were the baker's children. He had it tied to a string. He'd hold the edge of the string which the children called the *stitch* and the poor green-bottle tried to get away, to free itself from the string. The only thing it managed to do was to fly around in circles in the air like a top. It was a May-bug. Josephina, who was in Mrs. Maria's yard with her children, sympathized with the golden-green bug for its pratfall. She felt a strange shiver mixed with fright and disgust for all bugs and now this one here, had made her care about it. Above all she couldn't believe that the children were tormenting that little thing, making it their toy. The children, at least where Augusta's sister, Galatia, lived, usually searched for ways and materials to make their own toys which would keep them company, when, of course, they didn't play *hide* and *seek*, *chase* and *hopscotch*.

They'd make cars from damaged tires and spare parts that the grownups had thrown away or they'd find them outside the only car dealers in town, and the people who worked there would chase the children away because the materials they chose without asking weren't always unusable.

The girls on the other hand, would sew clothes for the only doll they had, from the rags the seamstresses would throw away. Anything the grown-ups threw away and the children found would become a game in their hands.

Once a year, though, at the bazaar and fair that were set up in the town's square, almost all children would buy something: a plastic doll with a spongy dress and plastic hair that was drawn on in brown, black or yellow and tin cars, wooden swords and kitchen utensils and sponge doves. The girls would also buy fake rings, lockets and crosslets. However, their bazaar toys wouldn't last very long, soon got broken so they saw to replacing them with makeshift toys and did so quite well! With improvised ones they did quite a good job of it.

Playtime there didn't resemble play time in the city. The children would all gather and would play all day long in one yard or the other. When they got hungry they'd leave for a while only to return holding a soggy slice of sour dough bread with sprinkled sugar on it. They were all friends until they quarreled and became the worst of enemies. Because they often did fight and then punches would fall or a stone pelting war would begin. Half the children were on the one brawler's side and half on the others'. Quite often, heads would crack open and noses would bleed and only when blood was shed or a mother came out and scold them would the stone pelting war end... not the fighting though. This persisted with swearing and threats.

Chapter 15   A green-bottle with a stitch.

At those times, Josephina imagined she lived in a pretty, strange fairytale. Everything was different there.

The children, the full time game the children had and played continuously from dusk to dawn, the grown-ups and the jobs most of them did, the way they all lived…

She could be walking in the street when a flock of impressive geese would suddenly appear in front of her, swaying from side to side, moving their necks and heads gracefully and rattling away in their language nonstop. They were farmed so the family could eat or were sold at the market which took place on Saturdays on the main street which divided the town in two. The geese would sometimes peck the children which was the why Josephine was afraid of them even more than the cows which no matter how big they were, were at least quiet and discreet.

The cows of the upper and outer areas would take to the road for grazing and returning, at dawn and dusk respectively. The cattleman or cowgirl was a man or woman from each neighbourhood who would take turns in leading the herd to the grassland and watching over them all day. Their responsibility lasted up to the time when the last cow would return home. When the first early morning bellows and cowbells were heard, the neighbors would open their gates for the cows to leave and mingle with all the rest which were coming. All of them knew the area well and very rarely would one miss its house on the return route.

IN THE YARD of the Paneons, Voula the eldest of the girls, would give Josephina a stool and would ask her to behave herself *"The cows need peace and quiet while being milked",* she'd say. Josephina knew that Canella, Voula's cow, could give a kick and spill all the milk Voula had gathered inside the wooden bucket, if the cow was startled by a sudden noise. Then all the milk and Voula's efforts would go to waste. Josephina said that Voula's bucket was identical to the one that the *milkmaid*[37] carried on her head; the milkmaid who was drawn on a label that covered the can of the sweetened condensed milk she drank. Not only could Voula not carry the bucket on her head but she even called her brothers to help her.

At the Paneons family everything was really different and she liked all of it.
The house itself, its things, its people, its animals, the way they lived.

It was mounted on a brownish, steep hill with sparse greenery and a big slope. They ascended almost climbing, there were small steps here and there but it wasn't clear if they had been carved out by a human or were carved naturally from the daily comings and goings of the family; it was located at the top of this steep hill.
On the inside it looked like train carriages because of the way each room communicated with the next, with two inner doors, one across from the other. Each room also had its own oblong, outer door and it was a rather low-ceilinged house; it was more than twenty meters long and five meters wide. It had three bedrooms, a dining room and a kitchen which the Paneons called a kitchenette, as it was a bit lower than the rest of the construction. The roof tiles were of terra-cotta shade.

---

[37] *The* famous *Milch Mädchen* (Swiss) on the cans of *Nestlé* sweetened condensed milk; *Milkmaid* in English, *La Lechera* in Spanish, *Βλάχα* in Greek...

Chapter 15   A green-bottle with a stitch.

The Paneons house was always clean and white on the outside, painted with fresh whitewash. There were wooden benches and countless clay flower-pots with marjoram and basil.

They ironed with a heavy black iron which they placed lit coal inside, and Voula's sister would wag it to and fro in the air and then she'd iron.

The butter they ate, they made themselves inside a tall, wooden, strange looking pot which looked as if it was upside-down because it was narrower at the bottom and wider at the top. There was also a strange looking pole which they used to softly beat the milk which slowly started to turn into butter after a length of time.

They washed their dishes and clothes adding a little bit of ash wrapped in a handkerchief and called it lye... Josephina never understood why they did this just as she never understood why they added ash, lye ashes to be exact, to the dough they kneaded once to make sugared shortbread. When she had asked Voula why, she had told her that she didn't know either; it was just the way she was expected to do it.

All these things that she never saw anywhere else, and which remained without explanation, made her want to stay in their home, such was the unusual fascination which it held for the little girl.

It was also the fairytales Voula told her. They were strange too, they all talked about goblins but Voula didn't call them that. She called them hobgoblins and hobs. The best fairytale was the one about a black, pitch black goblin who didn't have the heart to do evil to humans because he wasn't a fiend, not even a jackanapes, and that was the reason why all the other goblins chased him, but luckily never caught him.

Even the rooms in this house had their own distinctive smell.

The kitchen smelled of baked dough, bread dough, pancake dough, fried bread dough and dough for pies. Raw dough, baked dough and sometimes burnt dough, fried potatoes and eggs sunny side up. It also smelled of fried sausages.

At dusk, the whole house smelled of incense.
The grandmother of the family would go in and out of the rooms, censing "*so the old serpent would stay away from the house*" as she would say. Josephina asked over and over again who this old serpent was but nobody, not even Voula who told her everything, had ever offered an explanation.
From the inside of everyone's wardrobes, the smell of lavender and naphthalene would emerge when they opened their doors.

The boys' room often smelled of *tsipouro*[38] and *cognac*[39] and their sisters would pull the windows and doors wide open. In the girls' room it smelled of nail polish and acetone, rosewater and almond oil for their faces, hairspray and perfume depending on the occasion. In this room, the women of the house, who hardly ever went to the hairdressers, cut each others' hair and Voula had a lot of snail curls framed around

---

[38] Strong, distilled spirit, approximately 36°- 45° alcohol by value, produced by the residue of the wine press. Occurred 7 centuries before at the *Mount Athos Monasteries*.

[39] A variety of *Brandy,* named after the town of *Cognac* in France.

Chapter 15   A green-bottle with a stitch.

her face. She would take small tufts of hair and furl it inside cigarette papers which she then fastened with hairpins. Later on, when she'd unfurled it, her hair was full of carefree forelocks... and how they became her!

In the dining room, it smelt of soft vanilla sugared *loukoumia*[40] which they placed inside a special glass made covered tray.

As soon as the cold set in, then the whole house smelt of burning wood as the fireplaces were lit, one in each room as the winters up there were long and nippy.

The grandmother of the Paneons, who didn't remember how old she was, had her bed in the kitchenette. She demanded to have her covers changed every day and never allowed anyone to sit on it. However, there were plenty of times when Josephina would climb on the forbidden bed and would start jumping! This would be followed by the grandmother shouting *"take the lunatic off or the bed will break"* and Josephina, without ceasing her jumping would answer, *" no, I am not a lunatic"*, while Voula and the others would gesture to silence grandmother and to get Josephina off the bed. At that point Lazy the dog, who always slept under that bed, would wake up. He'd stretch and yawn, look at them one by one and would start to bark either at grandma or at Josephina.

Josephina who was afraid of dogs would then climb into Voula's arms and wouldn't climb back out! However, she cared for him and there were plenty of times when she'd

---

[40] Jelly delight of starch and sugar; in small cubes dusted with icing sugar. Can be found around the Mediterranean countries; although is a traditional Turkish delight, *Loukoumia* of the Greek island of *Syros* as well as those of *Cyprus* tent to be the most famous.

sneak into her pocket a piece of meat, cheese or a meatball so she could give it to Lazy, and Galatia tried in vain to find out how she got her pockets so dirty!

On one particular evening, Josephine was jumping on grandmother's bed again. As on other occasions grandmother scolded her, but this time however Lazy didn't bark at anyone, and Josephine went searching for him. He wasn't under the bed. They told her that he hadn't been seen since the night before, when he had gone out for his daily walk in the neighborhood... he hadn't yet come back and they were all worried.

STATHIS pretended to be the driver. He drove his imaginary car, speeding left and right on the cobblestone pavement, making the sound of the engine with his mouth. He wasn't holding anything in his hands, but he turned the non-existent steering wheel and changed the gears, which were also non-existent. He also overtook Velissaris who was driving the lid of his mother's brand new casserole. Surely he had secretly taken it!

"I bought a new car, do you like it?" he said to Stathis.

The two young drivers drove all the way to the water tank. They parked their cars on the ridge then they climbed and got onto the flat roof of the tank. It was grassy and smelled of fennel which grew on it. A bit further away something was beginning to smell bad. They started looking for *"the thing that smells"*.

It was poor Lazy, lying among the ferns... They clamped their hands over their noses and toddled off. They descended the ridge and chanced to see the heavy steel door of the tank...

Chapter 15   A green-bottle with a stitch.

open… That was strange… On their way they had bumped into the guard who had been leaving on his bicycle and he had actually said *"goodnight, boys"* which meant that his shift was over for the day. Had he left the door open? Oh… and there was the lock from which the key was hanging…

The two boys silently agreed, with a glance, to go inside.
They proceeded to do so… it was a huge square room, high-ceilinged, without a single opening on its walls. It smelled of dankness and fugginess. It was dark but there was an electric panel high on the wall beside the door. They agreed, again with a glance, to turn on the lights. Velissaris lent his back as an aid to climbing and Stathis jumped on it and reached the panel. There were many porcelain levers; they had to be the switch keys. He turned all of them into the on position and the room was lit. The snap of each switch had sounded terrifying. The dark huge square room became bright.
The watery environment was odd and gave out a sense of awe. They were standing on something that looked like a balcony, way above the level of the water. Flowing sounds could be heard in the void space. Echo and sound were all heard simultaneously. The same went for their footsteps which frightened them and they kept turning around to see who was following them. Stathis was on the verge of saying something but as soon as he uttered the first word, they both jumped. Stairs descended towards the area of the water storage. Water was rushing forcefully out of big spouts. Red lines and numbers on the walls showed the tank's water level. They could feel the dampness touching them. It was a mysterious environment which conjured up strange ideas.
They whispered into each other's ears because if they had talked out loud they'd become terrified again because of the

way it would sound, as if a thousand mouths were talking, one right after the other, continuously in repetition with the sole intention of terrifying the two young visitors. They looked at each other, silently agreed, and left the tank in a hurry.

They returned holding the dog. Velissaris went in front holding its two front legs, turning his head away in disgust. Stathis was holding its two hind legs with the one hand and with the other was holding his nose. They threw the dead dog inside the water tank. It fell with a splash, seemed as if it was about to sink but came quickly back up on to the surface. Velissaris lost his footing and nearly fell in with the dog and Stathis called him a *moron*. The word echoed over and over again as if a thousand mouths had uttered it. Velissaris started running like hell instead of getting mad that a thousand voices were calling him names. Stathis followed. Their own footsteps sounded as if they were chasing them.

The dog had remained in the tank, floating from side to side, doing its very best to contaminate the water that the unsuspecting locals would soon be drinking.

The children, like good home-makers, locked the heavy door and left the key in the lock. Each took their own invisible car, started up the engine and took off. They would have been scared to death if they had known that the Tank guard passed by only once every two days and if he had happened to remember that he had left the door open and had returned to lock it, he could have locked both of them inside for the next two days!

"Do you think that is what the ocean is like, Stathis? Like the Tank?" Velissaris asked innocently and full of curiosity, parking his car beside a milk thistle. *"How in heavens should*

Chapter 15   A green-bottle with a stitch.

I know? Have I ever been there? When I grow up, I'll work, make money, buy a car and go sea!" he laughed, squinting his eyes and added that his father wanted to make him a baker just like himself, but that he had already made his decision. He was going to become a teacher and nothing else...

The contaminated water started to hit the residents three days later, regardless of age. It played havoc on the children, though. The doctors searched for the mysterious cause. Stathis and Velissaris, the two young culprits who took more than half the town's population down, were also infected.

Galatia visited them in hospital. Stathis was rambling and his mother was crying, saying that her son was *bansheed*.

"...*the water is so much; wow! Such a lot of water! And the pipes are many! ...Velissaris, look, that's what the ocean is like... like the Tank! Let's go before the guard comes back... bring the dog... good idea to sink it... it won't sink... so much water... so much darkness! Watch out you moron...! You'll fall in too...! Come on, its dead, what harm can come to it if we throw it in...*"

But then she immediately understood what had happened. She advised his mother not to say a word to anyone about what the child had said so that they wouldn't get themselves into trouble. The children were young and naïve and had no way of knowing that their actions would cause an epidemic, but if word got around they wouldn't be able to get away with it, even if only one resident set out to formally charge them... Being married to a lawyer, her eyes had seen plenty...

JOSEPHINE had started asking questions from a very early age. The sort of questions that baffle the grown-ups. The ones that cause discordance and war. A war of conflicts and disagreements. *"Children must know! They must know the whole truth!" "Wrong! Children must not know the truth! At least not all of it! They ought to be protected!"* Augusta knew that she had to be really careful. *"Balance is always the same"*, she believed. *"Delicate and stretched like a tight rope. Ready to snap at the slightest maladroitness. Then, there's the truth. And the lie. The answers are there. Of course they're there... they don't come out easily though. At least not always."*

Josephine learnt that babies were either brought by storks, carried in their beak by the corner of their diaper but without anyone actually knowing where the stork had found the baby or that babies were found inside cabbages in the garden and again without anyone knowing exactly who had put the baby there... or that they were brought by a fairy -but again no one knew where she found them. She learnt that when a person leaves this world, he becomes a flower or a shooting star or a star that doesn't fall from the sky but stays way up high, pinned inside the clouds.

IT WAS THE first day of the school year; a short while after the blessing by the priest with holy water, and as soon as they entered the classroom and sat at their desks, - she would be sitting at the same desk as Little Kiki this year, too, she thought!- she was informed of the news, together with the rest of the children in the class. The teacher told them without beating around the bush. She didn't hide a thing. As bluntly as she could.

Chapter 16   Little Kiki, the one who left.

"Vassiliki was killed. She was run over by a car, this summer. She was squashed!" she had told them. She also added that the driver wasn't careful, Vassiliki wasn't careful, neither of them had been careful and so misfortune had come. The teacher had spoken boldly, certain that she was doing the right thing. She didn't speak of flowers, or shooting stars, not even of stars that don't fall from the sky but stay pinned in the clouds. She pitched their souls up against the wall and shot them before they could stand their ground. They all knew about such incidents before they ever spoke about flowers and stars. The flowers and the stars that Josephine believed in seemed hopeless and didn't stand a chance in pitting themselves against the sober tongue of the teacher.

A LITTLE while before November ended, Little Kiki with her honey colored eyes, the brown hair, the tall stature and the good manners, left too. The two little girls had been growing up together as their mothers had been friends ever since they were little, too. More often than not, they would dress their daughters in the same clothes, just like that November.

That Saturday night their new, woollen coats were ready. Yellow and white for Little Kiki. Almond green and white for Josephine. They were polo coats, with a big box pleat on the back and they buttoned up on the side with beautiful, golden, metallic buttons. Their others ironed both of them and had hung them up in their hangers. Constantia had taken Little Kiki by the one hand and the coat with the hanger in the other and had left.

The morning dawned. Little Kiki was beautiful in her canary colored coat with the golden buttons. She was between her parents who were holding her hands on either side.

"Josephine, won't you come with us to the parade?" she had asked happily. *"Come with us... they sell candy floss there!" she tried to persuade her.* Little Kiki's father, a calm, sweet, reserved and smiling idealist, wanted them to attend the patriotic celebration in Gorgopotamos[41] in order to honor some worthy ancestors...

They all set out with the best of intentions. At least that's what it seemed.
30,000 people from all over the country. Tanks and laurels. Marches and mass demonstration. National frisson and memorial service. Funeral wreaths and worship. Key messages and slogans. National pulse and idealists. Pure and impure. Brigades of people. Oceans of them. And police to keep the order. To clamp down on disorder.
And a formal representation of the government. The former and the current. These and those. 22 years after the bombing of the bridge for the pay off of a national debt. Guilty citizens and innocent citizens. A nicely organized patriotic fiesta. Nothing more.
Josephine was jealous. She wouldn't be going with Little Kiki. She even cried. The two little girls continued waving to each

---

[41] A celebration of the anniversary of the explosion of the Bridge of Gorgoporamos (10 km SW of Lamia); an Allient victory after the success of the sabotage Operation *"Harling"* on 25 of November 1942 during the WWII, in order to disrupt the supplies for the Rommel's troops in Egypt. A major success for S.O.E., which formed the demolition party. The operation carried out by the 12 British men of S.O.E. (2 of them were New Zealanders); the 86 guerrillas of ELAS by Aris Veloouchiotis and the 52 men of EDES military arm by Napoleon Zervas, provided cover and the main force of 100 guerrillas neutralized the garrison. Local people also helped in the way the men of S.O.E. asked them.

Chapter 16   Little Kiki, the one who left.

other until Little Kiki and her parents disappeared around the corner. Only then did Josephine stop crying and tear her little face away from the iron fence of the garden as she was certain that the situation would not change to enable her to go with them.

At noon, though, she started complaining to her father, hanging from his neck, but he upheld Augusta's decision. *"Your mother did very well to say no! Gorgopotamos... No way!"*

Lela looked at them uncomprehending. *"And why, my dear Sir do you consider that she made the right decision? With your permission Mrs. Augusta, the child cried her eyes out! She missed the parade! Would it have been so bad? I'm sorry to say it, but children like these things!"*

"Do you know what might happen there today, Lela? Slaughter is what might happen!" Mario continued.

"Slaughter? Heaven forbid! And who would slaughter who? It's only a parade!" and she immediately knocked on wood to prevent the evil omen that Marios had just divined.

"I know what I'm talking about! Do you think that up there today, everything will be rosy? That arguments and fights and assertions won't break out as to who blew up that bridge? Everyone today will want the victory for himself! They want to make a monopoly of the explosion, all of them. I know what I'm talking about! Don't be fooled by the fact that I don't get into political conversations! Today of all days is seething! Mark my words! Everyone will take advantage of the celebration but... will they all behave themselves? Or will they all be in different camps and go off the deep end?

These gatherings are NOT for children!" He addressed Lela, swinging his rolled up newspaper up and down. As soon as he stopped talking, at the precise moment when he was throwing his newspaper on to an armchair feeling aggravated, the sound of sirens ripped through the air on that quiet Sunday afternoon. The wailing of different sirens; those of the fire brigade combined with the sirens of the ambulances and the police sirens. Sirens that merged their dramatic wails in a hair-raising composition.

"Dear me!..... What's this?..... Could it be a proclamation of war? With the Turks? Or maybe the Third World War? It seems that great disaster has struck here! Lord have mercy on us!"

Lela was scared and started once more to knock on wood. When she stopped doing that, she began crossing herself. The neighborhood was becoming really restless and wired. The same could be said for the whole town judging by the voices and the car horns which filled the air. Augusta suggested calling the police in order to find out what had happened but the lines were continuously busy. They had tried to listen to the radio. Their ears caught something about blood bottles. They waited but heard no more. Beyond doubt something terrible had happened.

They left Josephine with Lela and asked her not to leave the house and not to lose countenance whatever information came to her ears. The people had already formed lines down both sides of the central street. Some had dashed out of their houses in fear, still wearing their pyjamas. Everyone's eyes were on the unusual locomotion of the street. The sirens continued to tear through the air. A medley of vehicles,

Chapter 16   Little Kiki, the one who left.

private cars, lorries, busses, tractors and motorbikes went by tooting their horns extensively. The first rumors started to go round. Some people spoke of a bus that had fallen in the river. While yet some others said that two buses had collided. While yet others, more sceptical, said...

"Something else is going on here, but what?" However, it was obvious that whatever it was that had happened, the majority of the vehicles, had one destination: the City Hospital. Everyone was in agreement on that.

The evil was finally revealed. It was painted in red. In blood. In the back of the open trucks the injured were transported. Hands were ripped off; legs... missing; eyes... pulled out; people unconscious; heads wrapped up extemporarily with shirts; bodies wrapped up in the same way; cloths drenched in blood. A blood curdling sight!

What on earth was going on? In Gorgopotamos, an explosive situation had been brewing there since morning. All that was left, was for it to be served. Around noon, the priests chanted for the souls of the fighters. Then the wreaths were laid. After that, things heated up. Each one sparked up for his own reasons. Some spoke of patriotic monopolies. Others about verdancy. The old land-mine made itself heard ten minutes after the departure of the officials. It didn't say much. At least not as much as it ought to have said so that everyone could understand from the start what had happened: Who brought it? Who placed it? Who triggered it? Why did he do it? If he did do it in the end and it hadn't been there for years, of all the past 22 years, waiting for a cause to detonate. The only thing it did was produce a single bang. A deafening one. One that jangled everyone's ears and afterwards, smoke started

rising. By the time the people there realized what had really happened; they thought that an enactment of the explosion of the bridge was part of the program.
For seconds, they concluded that yes, even though it had been very sudden and unexpected, it was moving to live -even through a re-enactment- the chilling moments of a patriotic sabotage that once made a fool of the enemy.

God help if it wasn't like that... and the thoughts remained suspended, coming and going in the smoke of the explosion which would also disperse in a little while. What sort of re-enactment were they even talking about!
In a revival of a scene, innocent people are not killed. In a representation at the very most, they use dummies... Did they mistake those people down there for dummies?
Bodies were mutilated. Heads decapitated.
Ululations and lamentations.
People who quailed for their own people. Plangent mourns. Voices -the same which a while ago shouted patriotic messages- were now asking for help. The wounded were writhing, spilling their blood on the land of Gorgopotamos. What sort of enactment was this? No, it was anything but a re-enactment! The people once more operated like a mob. Some *moduli* forever remain... *moduli*. Stoning for the police. And vituperations. Beatings in reciprocation. Riot. Chaos.
An eruptive situation, everywhere...

A reporter of the local paper would later write *"The more composed members of the crowd tried to intervene, in vain though..."*

The gonfalons go down before they are well raised. The blood of the child, which springs from a slashed neck, splatters the

Chapter 16   Little Kiki, the one who left.

people nearby. They scream in horror. It's Little Kiki's blood. She says *"mommy..."* and falls back. And panic. And horror. And terror. The parents don't know what to do. After the initial wailing everyone offers a helping hand. The little girl is transferred cursorily, lifted from hand to hand, through the midst of the masses of despair and the screams of anguish, into the back of an agricultural truck and from there to the hospital.

13 dead; Little Kiki among them.

51 wounded.

Fate? Who knows! May be so.

The helicopters transport blood from Athens. At least some will live. The luckier ones will make it... The local doctors are recruited. The peaceful town is mourning. The armed forces on guard. Too late now, as a danger foreseen is half avoided. The sirens continue their wailing. Some of these will be wails of salvation. It was the first time they had seen anything like this in the hospital. It all resembled a slaughter. Some kind of massacre. The expressions of *Why God?* and *No, God!* were engraved on everybody's faces. The traffic inside and out of the hospital was unusually heavy. Cars, people, cries, tears, car horns, policemen, wheelchairs and stretchers, swathed people, bloody flesh, cries of pain and sorrow. Orders and prohibitions, exasperation. Swearing from the indignant. Glum nurses, hasty doctors in a general climate of urgency. Everyone wanted something to overhaul. Even the evil. No matter that it had already happened.

LATE IN THE evening they told Josephine that Little Kiki had left for a journey. *"She'll be gone for a while"*, they told her.

"Why? Is this what was supposed to happen?" she asked.

The answer was affirmative. *"Yes, it is what was supposed to happen..."*

"She isn't going on a trip! I heard everything, I know everything! I heard it on the radio! Little Kiki is dead! The neighbors were talking about it outside! Her blood was shed, they said, wasn't it? Actually, Mrs. Maria said that she was drained of her blood, but Lela told me that it was spilled! It was a grenade, wasn't it? The thing that killed her... was a grenade, wasn't it?..."

The words bombarded Augusta one by one and all together like a catapult. Kneeling on the floor, holding her daughter's hands in hers, she gaped, her mouth open and her mind frozen, dumbfounded. How could it be that a small child could be spitting out such words so bluntly and dryly, without a single tear? Augusta was wondering if she understood each and every word she was using. Did she know what they meant? And if so, then, where did such a small child find this courage? Was it maturity or was she simply replicating everything she had heard? She dreaded to think that the child had heard all these details from the neighborhood. No matter how composed the little girl may have seemed, the wounds always work within the children and that's what Augusta was afraid of. The wounds of the soul, which aren't seen. Which come to the surface later on. When it's already too late.

"And I want to see her! Even with her head cut off! Her neck was cut, wasn't it?" Josephine continued to strafe.

"So, what happens now?" Augusta was on the verge of losing

Chapter 16 Little Kiki, the one who left.

it, especially because of the hair-raising imprecisions the little girl was blurting out. How much had she heard already?

"First of all, Little Kiki's head wasn't cut off" She began slowly and swallowed with difficulty but the lump that blocked her throat wouldn't go away. *"It wasn't cut off, I swear! Since you've heard everything, hear me out too, please! She only had a tiny cut... right about here... on the neck. Do you understand? And her blood wasn't spilled!"*

"Nor, drained?"

"No, sweetheart, it neither spilled, nor drained! None of all this! How can I explain it to you...? She... she just bled a little, that's all! A tiny bit! But she wasn't taken to the doctor quickly enough and that's why all this happened. They were delayed because there were a lot of people there! They couldn't get through! And don't listen to what the neighborhood is saying! They don't know what they're talking about! It's terrible that we've lost Little Kiki, I know. But nothing of what the neighbors are saying happened to her! She wasn't in pain. She didn't even feel it! And tomorrow I'll show you the newspaper! 'It was a land-mine' it'll say. The neighbors don't know anything so they're saying it was a grenade... and you will see Little Kiki! So you can see for yourself that her neck wasn't cut! And that her head will be there, in place! Promise me only that you won't think about what those silly women have said! And remember Little Kiki as she was." She looked her straight in the eye and tried to be as convincing as possible.

LITTLE Kiki's mother became mute. Forever. Her lips were never able to smile again. Ever. Her father kept all those poignant remnants of that Sunday well hidden. With him. Forever. Only for him.

He locked inside a narrow, long, metallic box, like a small case, Little Kiki's *Mary Jane* patented leather shoes, the ones she wore on the day she went away. And her three-quarter socks. And her ivory-colored dress, the one with the shirr in the waist and the bow that tied in the back, with the baby collar, the cuffed sleeves and the narrow ribbon with the strawberries and their leaves, which belted the hem-line all around, and Josephine was left to wear the exact same one all alone now. All of them drenched in blood. Her new coat was never found...

A dreary content, wrapped in a bunch of memories... Safely kept somewhere in the basement. So only he could open it, whenever he felt the need to hold his little girl in his arms and she wouldn't come... He'd unfold her clothes, tenderly and carefully as if they were made of glass and he was afraid that they'd break... He'd clutch them to his chest... Now, the only thing in danger of breaking was his heart. He'd kiss them, he'd caress them. He'd talk to them. He'd soak them with his tears. Then, he'd fold them again and put them back in their box. Again, slowly and carefully. With extra love and care. Just as every father should behave towards his child... The little key would turn. The small lock would continue to conserve its valuable contents. He'd dry his eyes. Caress the box. Put it back in its hiding place. On the last shelf behind the tool boxes. No one would look there. He struggled to find the heart to leave that basement. He'd caress it again. He'd say *"I'll be back tomorrow"* as if the box with its contents could hear him... and at last, he'd leave.

Chapter 16   Little Kiki, the one who left.

AT NIGHT Josephine would fall asleep listening to a fairy tale which was told or read to her usually by Augusta, Lela or grandfather whenever it was his year to stay with them.

"Lela, come tell us a story so we can fall asleep" she asked Lela that night.

"Tell y o u so y o u can fall asleep! There's only o n e of you, not ten!" Lela corrected her and the little girl explained that it wasn't only for her but for Little Kiki as well, because little Kiki also wanted to be told a story so she could fall asleep. *"Where Little Kiki is now, she neither wants nor hears stories!"* Lela ticked her off.

"Then, I don't want a fairy tale either!" The little girl got angry; she turned off her bedside lamp and buried herself under her eiderdown.

"I can understand telling y o u a story. For Little Kiki though? Where she is, she can't hear! She's a spirit! She doesn't need fairy tales!" Lela continued.

Josephine sprang out from under her quilt and jumped off the bed. She turned on her bedside lamp again. She got out into the hallway. She ran down the wooden stairs. In front of the bookcase, she climbed the steps of the ladder, which trailed on tiny wheels from one end to the other and hung from the top of the highest shelf. She seemed to know exactly what it was she was looking for. She hardly searched at all. She jumped half way down the ladder. She landed in a sitting position, holding a light blue book. She got up and started heading for her room. Her heels stepped on her nightgown.

She tripped. She lifted it, holding it in one hand and continued on her way up, stamping her feet on each step. She was in such a hurry that Lela couldn't imagine what her next move would be, so just settled for following her around as if she were her shadow. She got under her quilt again.
Lela stood beside her with her hands on her waist, looking angry. She still didn't know what the little lady of the house was looking for in the middle of the night and now she demanded an answer and Josephine seemed like she was about to give it.

"Lela, listen and never tell me again that Little Kiki doesn't hear, doesn't see and doesn't want any fairytales! I don't believe any of this! It's a lie! Little Kiki hears, sees and is sad about all the things you're saying about her! Listen, please!" She was talking seriously but her anger seemed to have subsided. She searched through the pages of the light blue book with the title *"On the big road"*[42] for a moment and found the page she was looking for. She had turned it down the corner of the page and started to read out loud.

It said that children don't die. That they become angels. That they spread their wings and go to heaven dressed in long light blue or rosy or white dresses, same as the clouds, and flutter around God's throne singing songs and playing the guitar. It spoke about a little boy who never told his family that he wanted to leave and neither had they seen any the indication of his growing wings on his small back. He left them, however. And mommy's knees emptied and her lap was void

---

[42] From the book *"On the big road"* by *Julia Da Vara* (1959, *Faistos* Publishers, Greece).

Chapter 16   Little Kiki, the one who left.

and the room was vacant of the small bed. And everything fell silent. However, he never entirely left their lives. It said that his sisters knew that the little boy, the tiny one who became an angel, would lean down from some place in the heavens and would look at them and when white clouds would passed by, they knew that he was in there, flapping his wings. And they would stand in front of the window, at nights, and would look among the stars in search of their little boy's eyes...

"I also look for Little Kiki's eyes among the stars. I haven't found them yet though, but I'm still searching... And the story, she hears it too! When the fairytale begins, Little Kiki comes. I know and her wings are very warm..."

"What nonsense is this, child? What wings and hooey? What wings?" Lela managed to say when the child's mother entered the room. Her daughter's fretful to-ing and fro-ing on the stairs had brought her to the bedroom. She had heard in every detail everything that had been said.

"Lela, go to bed! Tonight, I'll tell the girls a story! Josephine, are you both ready? What do you say? Shall we begin? Ok... Once upon a time..."

It wasn't the right time to give explanations and Augusta knew it. Of course, Lela didn't know this and so her eyes opened wide in surprise. She left the room, halted, returned, looked through the crack in the door and crossed herself. Within a few seconds Augusta had evaluated everything the little girl had said and decided to play along so that she could gradually help her emerge from the dream or maybe the nightmare. She herself didn't know whether it was a dream or a nightmare. She would give her the time and care she needed so she could grow accustomed to the loss and to the idea that nothing would ever be the same again for Little Kiki nor for Josephine in connection with her friend who had left. In the morning, she would explain to Lela too, who was now standing behind the door in the hallway, crossing herself and lifting her eyes to the heavens, asking for the help of the Virgin Mary. Help for Josephina and Augusta and for the crazy things the two of them were saying which she couldn't begin to understand.

Josephine fell asleep a little bit before Cinderella tried on her lost pump. It seemed to Augusta that the little girl was smiling. She caressed her hair and kissed her cheeks.

"My little girl, is it Little Kiki whom you're smiling at, I wonder?" she said softly and as she was carried away, she scanned the room with her eyes, from the floor to the ceiling...

Chapter 17   Grandma, Augusta's mother.

LELA WAS always hearing things at night. Hearing noises. Existent and non- existent. To her, the loneliness and solidarity of the nocturnal silence only enhanced the familiar sounds of the house. Especially when Augusta, Mario and Grandpa were not at home.

The ticking of the clock, the familiar cuckoo sound, coming from the little wooden bird at every change of the hour, the purring coming from the stray cat Josephina had picked up from the streets and which, when not hunting moths in the yard, would lie contentedly beside Lela's bed, purring happily. She would even be frightened by the reflection of the icon whenever light from the vigil candle wick, drenched in oil, wobbled; a light which the whole ceiling seemed to move under. This is why Lela would stay perfectly still, eyes wide open, staring right above her, where the white of the ceiling was ever an ochre yellow, and missed every opportunity to admire all that intricate embroidery that was spread out on the ceiling as the light came through the lantern cuts. And as if everything that went on in her room and, indeed, in the entire household -since there was a noise coming from the refrigerator or from a dripping tap from time to time- was not enough, there was also that rustling that seemed to come from every single tree in the garden. There was the sudden flight of the bats nesting in the citrus trees. There was the howling of a dog, even though the animal was far away, not to mention those stray neighborhood cats that wouldn't stop fighting all night. The moment Lela thought they were gone, they always returned chasing each other, meowing as if skinned alive, and never ceased fighting before the break of day.

At nightfall, all these things along with the familiar shadows of the household objects became a nightmare for Lela. A nightly, dark conspiracy oozed out of every little corner. She was startled even by the sound of her own footsteps. Even when barefoot, their echoing made her believe that someone followed her every step. And when there was a creak coming from the old wooden staircase leading from the ground floor to the bedrooms, Lela covered her head and held her breath, waiting to see who was coming up. Therefore, it was not wise at all to have her mind on a child, when she was afraid of her own shadow.

"She will drive the child crazy" worried Grandma, and had proposed to Augusta to let Josephina sleep over at her place, whenever she and Mario spent the evening out.

But the truth is that Lela loved to stay home alone. She'd dance to the rhythms of Elvis Presley and Adamo, holding tightly in her arms a pillow, or to the rhythms of the Beatles and Tom Jones, when the escort was the pole of the vacuum cleaner. She'd also try on Augusta's clothes, shoes, accessories and cosmetics and was singing in front of her mirror; she pretended she was Ann Marie David, Françoise Hardy, Sylvie Vartan or Rita Pavone.

But she also sang for hours the songs *"pour un flirt"*, *"petit demoiselle"* and *"teenie weenie yellow polkadot bikini"* and *"stasera mi butto"*. And of course she was afraid of nothing!

Chapter 17   Grandma, Augusta's mother.

JOSEPHINE was nearly eleven. That night, she was to stay at Grandma's. Lela would sleep -yet, the chances were that she would stay wide awake, surrounded by her nightly fears- with all the house lights switched on. Inside and out; as if they had a celebration. At least that's what the rest of them believed, but she would dance again and sing in front of Augusta's mirror, wearing her clothes, jewellery and cloths.

Grandma, on the other hand, had had her own protocol, for years now, which remained unaltered even when Josephina was sleeping in her own bed with her. Josephina loved sleeping in that big bed with Grandma, and so it was. It was a beautiful, huge, tall bronze bed, always perfectly polished, with beautiful renaissance pastel flowers, painted on small porcelain rosettes on the headboards. Grandma's pure white linen bed sheets, the handmade lace and the thin strings tied up in little bows on the side of the feather pillows, the sweet scent of lavender that softly wrapped her as she lay on them, all these things she liked, and she immensely enjoyed sleeping over. When she was younger, she liked to hop and bounce on that same bed and Grandma tried to make her stop by telling her that the bed would collapse, even that the wooden floor would collapse, but Josephina didn't believe any of this so she continued hopping and bouncing.

So, Grandma had a huge love for the radio stations of the whole wide world. To her, when the night fell, the Greek radio stations existed no more. Of course, she liked to listen to the Greek-speaking programs of radio stations abroad. She learned the news of the Greek people in foreign lands, whoever they might be, she also heard the opinions of others about Greece, or about things that happened elsewhere and hadn't become known here. She rarely, if ever, missed the programs of Deutche Welle, the Greek-speaking program from Moscow, the Voice of America, the program from Tirana or the BBC.

She fumbled with the buttons of her *Erres* radio that gleamed in the dusky room, glowing with its rare, orange light. And, as it gleamed close by her right bedside table, she easily brought the needle to where she wanted it. The semi-transparent display bearing the frequencies and the names of villages and cities were something she knew like the back of her hand. From Sofia and Bucharest to Lisbon, from Belgrade to Rabat. From France to the other side of the Atlantic. Then to Asia, Africa, and who knows where else. She used to say that the old radio was her company. She turned the button and its black needle changed KHz to the left and to the right. She checked out for Hodge, some Hodge, somewhere on the other side of the Aegean Sea. Grandma called that Hodge a *Turk*. She also looked for music and African drums and broadcasts from the lands of the Sheiks, even though she didn't understand a word those people said. Sometimes she would murmur a chorus of far away Latin American melodies that filled her room. At other times, she softly swayed her head and shoulders to the sound of the Viennese waltzes, half-lying on two of her four puffy, feather pillows.

No matter where her *Erres* needle stopped, no matter which corner of the world overflowed her room, whether there was an aria or a madrigal, a dialogue or even a monologue, whether she understood the words or not, Grandma fulfilled her dream. A dream that was never meant to come true and seemed to come alive in the dim light of her room, like a

Chapter 17   Grandma, Augusta's mother.

romantic, unfulfilled fantasy: *Travel round the world!* This had been her heart's desire, ever since she was a little girl back in her maiden house. She craved for this same thing - even if she dared not utter it to anyone- even when misfortunes came upon her, one after the other. It was this same illusion that softened the pain at nights for her husband, who lived in exile, on the tiny Aegean islets. This same radio consoled her after his death, later on. It was only in front of this radio that Grandma allowed her tears to fall, in the evenings. Her children were not to see her cry. Not ever. And she wouldn't fall asleep if before doing so she didn't hear that *something* from the far ends of this world.

And Grandma did travel round the world, through the magic waves of her radio antenna that instantly placed the whole wide world at her feet. But, when she turned the button to its *off* position, she knew it wasn't for real, and bitterness overwhelmed her. But, luckily for her, there were also those times when she fell asleep like a baby without realizing it and the radio kept playing all night. At those times, Grandma didn't have the time to realize that the tour around the world through her bedroom, only existed in her mind...

That night, the candle lamp shone its orange light from up in its corner, high, on the ceiling, above the wooden chest. It was mysteriously pouring its sweet, soft light, ornamenting the larger part of the ceiling and two whole walls, until it faded halfway across the wall above the chest. One shutter was wide open. The house was raised about two meters from the ground, but there was no reason for particular precaution. It was, after all, surrounded by a fence at least two and a half meters high, with railings and blooming wisteria all around.

There was always a passer-by, or a passing car, not to mention the fact that the house was in the heart of the city. The night was lucid, transparent, and the star lit sky seemed to stretch from one end to the other, crystal clear. One after the other, the constellations had assumed their positions in the empyrean, and shone softly yet brightly from above, enhancing the clarity and brightness of the evening. It was a pity to sleep, on a night like this, and an even greater pity to try to fall asleep in a darkened room, lit by a night light at the very best, and keep outside one's shutters this beautiful night and the sparkling silver of the full moon, that were unleashed to sweeten the senses.

The two of them were laying under the white linen, their backs leaning on the feather lavender-scented pillows. They seemed quiet, silently enjoying the wonderful night. The bronze bed was shining in discreet luxury, and Josephine recalled that once, when she had commented on this, she had received from Grandma the answer that it is very unbecoming for bronze and silver items to be left dim and unpolished.

The distant, round shape of the full moon was now right outside their window. It shone through the white, semi-transparent cotton curtains and Josephina asked if they could be pulled aside, so she could have a better view of the moon. As soon as the curtains were pulled aside, Josephina's glance travelled from the moon to the ceiling, high up where the icons were kept. She asked Grandma why she kept her wedding wreaths among the icons behind the orange vigil candle.

"Because I wanted everything to go well with my marriage...

Chapter 17   Grandma, Augusta's mother.

I left them there, for the Virgin Mary to protect them..."

"And did she? Did she protect them?" She received no answer, just a long *"Shhh..."* from her Grandma, placing her finger on her lips. The silence was softly filled by sweet madrigals.

Grandma explained vaguely *"It is a European radio station!"*

Then, she moved the needle without even fumbling, since she knew the display of her radio by heart, connecting to the Vatican Radio. Well, Josephina knew all too well that she wasn't even supposed to breathe. Grandma would say her much loved night prayers, along with the Catholics. It didn't matter one little bit that she herself was no Catholic -she would repeat with them all fifty times *"Ave Maria... Santa Maria..."* The prayer of the Catholics which had been coming from the Vatican radio station to Grandma's room for years now. Every night. At the same time. Grandma had learned that prayer by heart. Word for word, without ever knowing exactly what it meant. To be honest, she had no idea of what these Latin words meant. She would recognize *Amen* for what it was, as she was certain that *Ave Maria* and *Santa Maria* were evocations to the Virgin Mary, and this she had understood because she was certain of *Maria*. In the beginning, many years ago, when she had heard this prayer for the first time, she set to counting the times it was repeated. She always counted fifty repetitions and so it was. *"It is a prayer, it must say something good. And Catholics are Christians, like us. And after all, they are human too. They must be praying to the Virgin Mary for the same things we are!"* thought Grandma, without ever telling anyone, out of fear that the prayer should lose its dominant charm.

LILY TSONI

Ave Maria, gratia plena, Dominus tecum.
Benedicta tu in mulieribus,
Et benedictus fructus ventris tui, Jesus.
Sancta Maria, Mater Dei,
ora pro nobis peccatoribus, nunc,
Et in hora mortis nostrae. Amen.

Josephina stayed awake, counting on her fingers the times the prayer was heard right through to -the fiftieth. She listened to her grandma repeating along with the Catholics and she was filled with pride. She promised herself that she, too, would learn such long and foreign prayers.

"After all, the Lord can only feel pleased that his children pray in peace and unity and make common prayers." she thought. She herself felt once more the weird, nocturnal bliss just by listening to that choir of the Vatican, even if she didn't understand what the words meant. *"As if I understand everything I read in the Bible..."* she thought again.

At the point then, Grandma yawned. She turned the black button to its *off* position, the radio stopped transmitting and the display with the yellowish lights, the cities of this world written in Latin together with their frequencies of its far ends, all marked vertically and horizontally, darkened. As if nothing of all this had ever existed in the room. The rhythmic ticking of the clock could still be heard behind the closed door. Faint as it was, it still kept you awake.
The warm, pleasant, translucent, Mediterranean night of May under the moonlight was still to blame. Sleepiness kept giving place to reflection.

Chapter 17   Grandma, Augusta's mother.

"I could write a very beautiful composition about this night" crossed Josephina's mind. In the garden's little stone-made pond, a little frog would not stop croaking. Somewhere nearby, a night bird gave out its solitary cry. Right across the street some cats were fighting and the neighbor's trained guard dog threatened them, as well as a passer-by whose footsteps you could hear on the cobble stone pavement -a job well done for a guard dog. Farther away, outside the city, near the river, came the sound of occasional shots from the hunters -who knows what they could be hunting, since, at this time of the year all hunting had officially ceased until autumn. From the far end of the valley one could hear the *cannons*, placed by the rice-growers to scare the otters, whenever they dared to raise their heads above the surface of the waters.

The train was heard passing by, whistling through the mountain tunnels. If one looked that way, it could be seen, distant, crawling in and out of the tunnels.

It was the night rout of the *ACROPOLIS*, going abroad. Still, it was as if something was missing from all these sounds of the beautiful nightly concert, and it was provided by the city clock, striking midnight which was heard from high up on the cathedral steeple. Its twelve strokes were anything but annoying, since the beautiful, sweet and full sound could not be heard during the day because of all the other city sounds. Two passing cars hit on the brakes suddenly, beeping too, in a strong, long, magnificent appoggiatura[43]. Their drivers drove away only after cursing and swearing at each other.

---

[43] Italian in text: *a leaning note (appoggiare: to lean)* that creates one of the dramatic events of the sonata form. A melodically important musical ornament, the most popular and important of the essential graces during the *Renaissance* and early *Baroque*, was notated inconsistently even in the late 18th century.

LILY TSONI

"I'm not sleepy, grandma!" the little girl said.

"And I thought you would be dreaming already! And what would you have us do? Any ideas?" she consented.

"Tell me about Grandpa! That is, if you want!"

"Hmm... oh, ok then, I will!"

She put the blankets aside and sat up, pulling her long white nightgown down, covering her legs to the ankles. Then, she took off the night cap and Josephina remembered that, this white puffy sleeping cap that Grandma wore to bed and tied it under her beautiful, although aged chin, reminded her of that other cap in the fairy tale, which was worn sometimes by Little Red Riding Hood's grandma and sometimes by the big bad wolf itself, pretending to be the girl's grandma. She giggled. She felt ready to burst into loud laughter, but bit her lips and didn't. Grandma only wore that cap when she was sharing the bed with her granddaughter, so that *"my hair doesn't touch the child's little face"*, as she put it. It would be rude of Josephina to laugh, and quite a shameful thing to do. Grandma switched on the lamp, stepped into her slippers, stood up and headed to the dresser. She drank all the water she had filled her glass with for the night and filled it halfway with some of her own home-made or geat, that she kept in there. Above the dresser there were a lot of photograph frames, silver, alpaca and tin, each with a tiny bow around the nail from which it hung. They were mainly pictures, from the old times.
She unlocked the two-leaved, recessed wall cabinet. Its key, a little green tuft hanging from it, was always kept in the

Chapter 17   Grandma, Augusta's mother.

pocket of her gown.
She took out a wooden box that resembled a jewellery case.

"She's going to show me her jewels! And maybe give me one!" she rejoiced.

It wasn't a jewellery case, though, or, even if it was meant to be, Grandma didn't use it as such. It was full of envelopes, and letters.

"It is probably her correspondence" she thought, but she would have preferred it to contain jewellery which she would examine, together with her grandma, even if she wasn't to be given any. They were tied up in four different packs, each of them with a cream, satin ribbon. She counted three more, all tied up the same way. Those contained photographs.

"Here, Josephina! Look at what a grandfather you would have had, if only they had let him be with us... you can, you can understand a man better through his writings..." And she placed a pack in her granddaughter's hand. She untied the ribbon. Took out two random envelopes. Both enclosed letters to Augusta, from her exiled father.

"Please read them aloud, so I can hear too! Although I have read them so many times that I've learnt them by heart!" said Grandma, and sat in her armchair, her feet on the stool, and her shawl around her shoulders.
Josephina jumped out of bed, she sat on the wooden floor with her back against her Grandma's armchair, and started reading.

LILY TSONI

First letter.

Lapsachades[44], 6-8-47
Good morning, Augusta, my girl! I am in good health, and I hope this find you the same.
Augusta, I received two letters, registered and included the photograph. In your letter you mention having sent two parcels, yet neither have arrived yet. Things are now being settled, so they should be here any time now. You write that some people have been dismissed. It was said that the Committee passed them on medical grounds, but sadly... They are being dismissed only because they know people in the Government. I also received a letter from your uncle Demos which I replied to. Nevertheless, for the majority of people it all depends on how the situation will evolve. So, we are playing a waiting game.
In your other letter, you wrote about the railroads and Michailides, but you didn't clarify the details. I can only imagine the kind of terrorism that reigns now! Write a little more each time, so that we know what is going on in our country. There is no censorship in letters. I wrote to Raphael again and to Papayannis, I will write to Tsekouras too and to whoever else owes me. I understand that something can be done. What bothers me is that the shop has gone out of business, but it was only to be expected, after all that has happened. Here, we are now sheltered in a chamber, and day after day we see to ameliorating our living conditions, preparing for the coming of winter. They promised us that they would try to improve the provision of food, as well. I still have money, 100 thousand drachmas. As for the

---
[44] In the Aegean island of *Ikaria*.

Chapter 17   Grandma, Augusta's mother.

company, all us the fellow citizens are together, except for a dozen or so who were scattered to the several villages where they had relatives. The rest of us stick together and so the time passes. Do not worry one bit. I will be as fine as the next person so do not worry! Please write and tell me, were those kept in detention released or not? As for Charamis, I succeeded in bringing him here to stay in the same place as me; we are also close friends with Charalambus..."

"Well... see your Grandfather, Josephina? He addressed himself to your mother in his letters since she handled most of the correspondence, but he cared about the entire family. He cared about his fellow prisoners.
He also cared about our finances, even though he himself was in need of a thousand things. He was reassuring us, while he was in need of reassurance himself. He was full of compassion for everyone..." said Grandma, and nodded to Josephina to go to read the second letter.

Second letter.

Evdilos[45], Island of Ikaria, 19-9 -47

Good morning! Rejoice, Augusta, my child!
I'm fine, Augusta, and kindly be informed that I passed the doctor's examination and have been released! We are now awaiting for the Sunday ship from Evdilos to Piraeus. Do not worry. So far though, I haven't managed to get that parcel with the trousers and whatever else was in it. I have received only two parcels, which I had written to you about

---

[45] Also in the Island of *Ikaria*.

in a previous letter. Now, you should go to the Post Office and fill in a return-to-sender application, but you have to have the receipt and its number in order for it to be properly returned to you. I have no more news to share. I embrace you all. Your father Eutihios.

ALAS, THE jour-fix[46] between Grandpa and freedom was still far way, as her Grandma explained to her. That *next Sunday* was not so near. The release only came for him six months later, a Pyrrhic[47] victory for Grandpa and his family... The much anticipated return for everyone, a dream he saw come true, was followed by two years of Grandpa, who was ill due to the hardships of the accursed exile, being bedridden.

Grandma remembered that "*... for two years, that is, as long as Eutihios lived, Dr. Stefopoulos visited twice every day; in the mornings before going to his office and in the afternoons, either before reopening or later in the evening, when he had finished his job. Never did he accept payment, either for the visits to tend your grandfather or for the medication he himself provided and gave to him.* "It is a shame, he used to say, to take money from Eutihios! You

---

[46] French in text: *fixed day*. A fixed day (weekly or monthly), giving the opportunity of participating in conversations, presentations or performances. A *jour fixe* is not open to the public and is mainly referred to cultural or artistic teams of people.

[47] A victory gained at too great cost; with heavy losses on the victor's side, as to be ruinous. Named after the King *Pyrrhus of Epirus,* after the battle between Pyrrhus's army and Romans' army (279 BC, Apulia -Italy- at *Asculum*); Pyrrhus was the Great Victor but he lost a great part of his forces, his friends and commanders. The term is used in popular culture in fields such as politics, business, sports and many others, when the cost of a victory or an achievement, is devastating to the victor.

Chapter 17   Grandma, Augusta's mother.

seem to forget that he is my best friend!" He examined him every day, he brought news from the city, he told him jokes to lift his spirit, he kept him company. He always took his morning coffee here, beside Eutihios. I can still see him as if it were yesterday! Tall and jaunty despite his age, his round spectacles, the grey beard and the hat, just like Eleftherios Venizelos... do you know who Eleftherios Venizelos is?" Josephina nodded that she did.

Then Grandma gave to Josephine a card-postal from the packs that contained photographs. It was a panoramic aerial view of a beautiful city crossing by a river and continued "... here is where my brother Nicolas lived..."

"Grandma, wasn't Nicolas the one who..."

"... who passed away two years ago, yes, that was him..."

She told her a great deal about Nicolas. That he was clever and restless, bold and capable of dealing with whatever he was involved in.
Moreover, he found favor with his father, who saw that he was never short of money.
So, he studied Economics and Commerce at the University of Grenoble.
She told her that he was an excellent student.

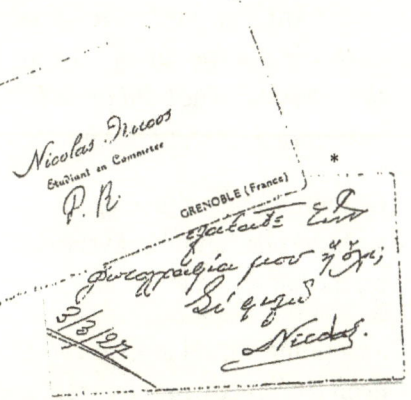

---

* 3/3/1927 "Have you received my photo or not yet? I embrace you, Nicolas."

After his studies, he became an aristocrat's mentor for a while, and this is how he acquired his first money, along with important and useful acquaintances. He turned to the practical side of what he had learnt. It was then that he stopped asking for money from his father. He started trading coffee to begin with, then started to export and later on was found to be the owner of two coffee factories, one in French Morocco, but the other Grandma couldn't remember where. However, one of them was burnt to the ground *by the niggers*, said Grandma, yet Nicolas built it up again. He was flourishing. Her Grandma mentioned proudly that he was also very handsome, but right at the point where she seemed so proud of him, dark shadow passed across her eyes. She told her that, for as long as he had lived in Greece he had been quite sensitive... and when he left, he was barely eighteen years old. He was still a boy, she said. Yet, he never showed any signs of nostalgia for his family, all those years.

"Not all was fine here in Greece, no doubt... nor were the opportunities as plentiful... but his family was here... didn't he even once miss his mother? She died with his name on her lips... And my father, who was so very fond of him, lived with his photographs... I too, have the same question all these years. What did or didn't Nicolas feel for us all. Here, have a look at him! See how well he had done for himself!"

Grandma's face shone again and handed her one of the packs with the photographs. Every photograph had explanatory notes on the back, and at the end, essentially, a signature. "*Nicolas*".

Josephina would stop at the French words, unknown to her even if correctly pronounced, and would look at her Grandma who would translate them for her. The French words had

Chapter 17   Grandma, Augusta's mother.

previously been translated to Grandma years ago, whenever such mail arrived from France, by Mademoiselle Marie, the French teacher who still lived next door and taught in the city.

"From the Soirée[48] de Gala held for the Greek Ambassador."

"During a thé dansant[49] at our country house in Chateau de Loire and bear the mind, it is worth sending me the children for summer holidays over here, they would love it!"

Of course Grandma's priorities were somewhat different to sending her children to the Chateau de Loire for the summer, but Nicolas couldn't even begin to imagine, as she told Josephina. She was too proud that she had never explained their financial and familial status to him. Even when her husband was ill in bed and her family's needs were great she never asked for his help or compassion.

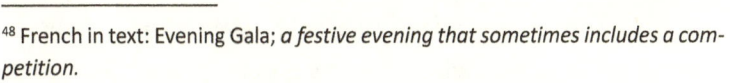

"Francoise, at one of her matinée[50] with her friends. Have I told you that she loves it when I speak Greek to her, and that she wants to meet you all?" He never brought Françoise over to meet them, as Grandma explained.

"Look at Françoise! Isn't she a doll?"

---

[48] French in text: Evening Gala; *a festive evening that sometimes includes a competition.*

[49] French in text: (First known use in France, 1819); *tea dance held in the late afternoon.*

[50] French in text: (First known use in France, 1856); *social/public event, held in the daytime;* from *Matuta,* the Latin goddess of morning.

"Hunting with my friends!"

"Horseback riding with Françoise!"

"Our house in Grenoble!"

"Better than the king's palace, I thought when I first saw this photograph!" commented Grandma and added *"But that other house by the river, the one that looked like a castle, I liked that one more!"* The truth is that it didn't *look like a castle*... it was a castle!

"Our household staff. We've had them for over ten years and we consider them family." And he explained that the black servant dressed in a cloak and the black cook with the turban had followed Françoise from her maiden home, and that their blond car-driver was German and their gardener French.

And of course, photographs of Nicolas outside his factories surrounded by the personnel, as well as inside the factory premises, near the machinery in the heart of the production... and naturally in his office holding a cigar, with a photograph on the wall behind him. Nicolas had that photograph made into a black and white portrait, and it showed their father on his horse. Perhaps, the only sign of Nicola's roots, which, according to Grandma *"meant something."*

The fancy photographs, the even fancier notes on the back of them, the ease that Nicolas appeared to have with everything, had made Grandma believe he was a wealthy man. Although they were brother and sister and blood is thicker than water she never once had asked anything from him, in all these years. Not the slightest little thing!

That Easter he sent his season wishes from Casablanca

Chapter 17   Grandma, Augusta's mother.

written on the back of a Christian Easter greeting card, depicting two young shepherds, grazing their few sheep with halos around their heads, resembling Jesus and John the Baptist. "*Heureuses Paques*"[51] was imprinted with golden, embossed letters, on the grass.

"It is the third time I ask you about your finance but you don't answer to my question! I am transferring some money; a small gift for children. Is Eutichios still ill? Please, inform me in details. From what I understand, even though you never mentioned it in any of your letters, you never had father on your side. Of course, you should have seen it coming, since it was a mésalliance...[52]
Everything will be better. You will see. Everything will be fine. I embrace you all, your brother
Nicolas."

She never received anything. Many years later, being his sole living relative, she was notified of his death by a French advocate. There was also a cutting from a French newspaper, informing its readers of the death of the prominent Greek. The advocate informed her that the deceased had left all his fortune to French almshouses. He had divorced the beautiful Françoise a while before.

"I didn't mind him not helping me out. I did perfectly fine on my own. He may have had his own problems which he didn't wish us to know of. What matters the most is that, for thirty

---

[51] French in text: *"Happy Easter Day".*

[52] French in text: *marriage with a person of different social status / inferior social position.*

two long years, he didn't come back even for a day! ...as if he had completely erased his past! Oh, and please don't blame him for the French words. Nicolas didn't forget his language, not even for a moment! Here, see how correctly he wrote? And it is quite difficult to translate all these festivities into Greek! See?" It was obvious that she would not have even a hint of blame attached to her brother's name.

"This beautiful little girl here, is this you, Grandma?" The yellow *fond-perdu* photograph showed a smiling little girl up to three years old. She had her hair braided and put up in a *"meatball"* over each of her little ears, and she was smiling over a huge, lace collar. In a full-length photograph, the little girl sat on a bench with a puppy in her arms. Her hair was neatly parted on the side and it was decorated with a white bow. She wore a long dress and over that, a loose, sleeveless old fashioned pinafore.

"This is our Virginia! My little sister!"

"I didn't know you had another sister! And now, where is she? What have you done with her?"

"Hmm, what have we done with her! We lost her! Forever! Our caretaker was cleaning his riffle. We kept three or four of them at home. Back then, everybody kept some kind of weapon at home, aside from the fact that my father also went hunting. Our little girl was running around, playing with her shadow, which the sun caused to dance back and forth, right and left. My father was quietly smoking his pipe. My mother was fastening my hair into braids.
Nicolas was secretly preparing birdlimes in the barn, because mother didn't allow him to do this. As for Giannis -

Chapter 17   Grandma, Augusta's mother.

my older brother- was somewhere in the neighborhood. Virginia popped in front of the bore of the gun. No one expected it. No one was able to prevent it. A sudden "bang" was heard. And the scream of the caretaker, and the sound of the gun falling to the ground as he threw it away, frightened. We saw Virginia miss her step, seconds before she fell on the paved yard. The caretaker had accidentally shot her down. So we lost our little girl. After the first shock, the caretaker jumped on his horse and fled. No one ever saw him again, nor learnt anything about him. Not even his own mother, whom my parents remained close to. How on earth were they to blame, anyway? I tell you, those were strange times. Strange were the people, too. Strange and cruel. My father kept that old woman. Me, he never let me in the house again. "My door is closed to you!" he had said to me... Sometimes, Josephina, in the evenings, it seems as if I am holding my little sister on my lap. I imagine talking to her, and she holds me tight, her little hands around my neck, as she did back then. Almost sixty years have gone by, yet I still hurt over that little girl's loss..."

Josephina was certain that her Grandma had a thousand reasons to feel bitter. But she never showed it. Josephina was also certain that her Grandma was a special, important, significant lady.

Grandma also remembered pleasant things. She remembered the two-storey, stone mansion where she was born and raised; with the large yard, the guest house, the servants' rooms, the cellar and the stables. Its chimneys smoked all year long. It seemed to Josephina that her Grandma could almost smell the roast meat and the fresh-baked bread. She remembered how much she enjoyed hiding in the closets where they kept the jars with the salted pork, with the grownups looking for her everywhere. Once, they had even locked her up in that closet, by accident. She remembered the sausages in the pork fat, in which they preserved until the following Christmas, and how she would secretly open the jars and eat from the raw sausage and pork fat, ignoring the grownups who had told her it would be as *heavy as lead* on her stomach.

She remembered her mother shoving potatoes, apples and eggs under the cinders of the fireplace, on endless winter evenings, and how they, slowly roasted and smelt heavenly. She remembered the two enamel teapots, the red one for cocoa, the blue one for herbal tea, always on the huge kitchen fireplace, where there was room for five iron gratings, the spit forks and a whole lot more.

Grandma even remembered her own grandfather, arguing about smoking with his wife.

"My grandfather would even smoke when on horseback...!"

"But, Grandma, I still don't know why my Grandpa went into exile!" Josephine interrupted her.

"And I was wondering whether you would ask! Firstly, Grandpa didn't go into exile. He was sent! There is a difference! And I will now tell you why... They assigned to your Grandfather the contract for the carpentry works in the new hospital. He was the lowest bidder and so he took the job. But another man wanted that contract, too. And he was mad at your grandfather, and he set out to steal this job from him. To do away with your grandfather once and for

Chapter 17   Grandma, Augusta's mother.

all! Because your grandfather was always entrusted with good jobs... that day his competitor threatened him in public, saying that he would never let him hammer a single nail into the wall! He nacted on his threats and your Grandfather found himself thrown into prison before he knew what was happening! And from prison, he was sent to exile, as a communist! He wasn't a communist, of course! But, as I've told you before, those were strange times. Strange, and cruel. It was easy to accuse anyone of something, and that person could not even defend himself!

There were "us" and "them", the good and the bad ones. Adults, playing recklessly and small heartedly, like foolish big babies, the game of civil war. Exactly so, my little one. Without caring whether households and families were being orphaned as a result! It was then that our torment began. For your Grandfather, mostly.
In the beginning, I found myself with my back against the wall. But I grew stubborn! I let nothing get me down! For my children's sake, above all else! I took all of our lives in my hands. I wouldn't let the enemy rejoice at our misfortunes. And I managed to do it. I worked hard. I kept a business that I didn't have a clue about before that day, and I before your grandfather died, it finally began to show signs of being prosperous.
"Well done, you did it!" he had said to me..."

The truth is that Grandma had also managed to create a strongly bonded family. Not like those which appeared bonded only in front of a photographer's lens... her household was full of love. Thus, it did not merely look beautiful... it was!

LILY TSONI

That night, Josephine felt as if she had grown a little older... was it because, for the very first time in her life, Grandma had spoken to her as if she were a grown woman, even though she was still a little girl?

And I no longer...

And I no longer...

give haircuts to the flowers of the garden and the muguet are my favourite.

I have been driving for years and I am a good driver, may be as a result of driving in the junk yard with the broken down deserted cars next to my neighbourhood...

I dance quite well but not better than those I had once watched dancing.

Elenitsa is now Mrs. Eleni and I'll always love her but we rarely meet nowadays... Since little Kiki left, I have seen her only once or twice, and those times in my dreams...

Grandpa and Grandma, who adored me, have been resting in peace for years now...

LILY TSONI

My father was Marios; I mean... Panagiotis, Josephine's daddy...

And in my mind I believe that I'm still searching with him for the bread crumbs that Le Petit Poucet threw in the forest... And that's how it must be, or else how could I explain it otherwise when I wake up and feel the warmth of his hand in mine, holding me tightly so I am not afraid in the heart of the forest?

And I am still searching, when the wild geese fly by, to distinguish whether or not their flock is still lead by the same leader, Akka from Kebnekaise...
Then I hurrently seek to make out Iksi and Kaksi, Kolmi and Neljä,
Morten the White male tame Goose, Viisi and Kuusi.

And I no longer...

The caravans with the gypsies have ceased coming. Achilles, Netos and Simos are fully grown men, now. I wonder, have they kept their hoops and their push scooters? Has Simos kept his stilts?

It seems that I only remember Old gal Voula and Shorty Urania.

What wouldn't I give to sit still on my wooden stool so as not to scare Canella – the cow Voula would be milking...

Who knows, do Stathis and Vellissaris remember me at all?

I would also like to know what has become of the women with the multicoloured rose-patterned carves?

Every so often I catch myself playing "the Glad game" that Pollyanna taught me. In the bookcase, there isn't a book missing from the Lilika -or Martine it doesn't matter at all- series!

Whenever I am in Lyon, I always dash to the second floor of Musée des Beaux-Arts, to stand in front of Gericault Mad Woman's portrait. Last time, the guard of the museum looked at me strangely when he heard me calling her "Maria"! Am I to blame that she is identical to poor Maria, Aristides' sister, of my childhood years?

I also go to Grenoble and try to distinguish my grandma's brother in the crowds, and when I find him, he takes me in his arms and cries: "Bienvenue!" and

And I no longer...

I start asking him why he never came back, not even once in so many years...
So, well Yes, I am Josephine, the white, the black, the yellow and the red! And I'm not kidding at all!
Here are the organdies my mother used to sew for me... you can also ask Lela, who even now passes outside Kassiani's house reciting the Lord's Prayer, even though that house has been demolished and another has been built in its place...
Lelaaaaaaa!!! Tell them!!!...

LILY TSONI

ACKNOWLEDGEMENTS

Without the help of some important people, "Josephine the black, the white..." would never have turned into the book in your hands. Therefore, I would like to offer my thanks to a number of people...

First and foremost, if I should thank anyone at all, who has helped me bring to life the lines that I wrote, who else but the very person, who gave me the inspiration, so... Alexandra, thank you!

My very best friend, Greek Italian Alexandra Christopoulou – De Palo, a Greek Italian fashion designer in Italy, created most of the drawings of "Josephine the black, the white..." Alexandra carefully monitoring and

Acknowledgements

faithfully recording my descriptions of the characters of my novel – who were real people that I may have known, but whom she had never met before– succeeded, in capturing on paper the essence of their appearance and style, as if they were photographic images! With she herself on the one side of the Adriatic and I myself on the other, we managed by means of the telephone to convey descriptions and assign corrections of the sketches.

We often resorted to urgent postal correspondence, emails within the wild early hours and unexpected changes to the original plans, and alongside and very occasional minor disagreements on finer details, I was able to ensure that the real heroes were brought back to life within the pages of "Josephine the black, the white..."

Below the line: But I myself had to make some small, artistic adjustments to some of the drawings of Alexandra as a consequence of certain changes that I had made at the very last moment in the text, and there was no luxury of time to ask Alexandra to make even the slightest change to the sketches.

It was then that either the idea was born over the unfolded plan while I was on a plane with no possibility of contact either a little more when standing side by side with the editor we send of the work for printing, and she no longer needed to count backwards to work out my local time.

So, this is my Achilles, who is now trying to hide himself behind the grandfather, who in turn had been

Acknowledgements

painted by Alexandra; and I drew him as I sat on the plane, because early in the morning it would take its place in the text.

That very same morning I changed the hair and shoes of Dominique, for strictly technical reasons, because something was wrong and it had to be done.

Finally, I had to dress Joan in Mary Quant designs guided by a specific photo of a distant collection of the British designer, that had caught my eye on most recently visit to the London haunt in Sloane Square. I also had to devote attention to the change in Joan's hair style and wardrobe on the spot, and more over I was in a hurry... so, Alexandra, please accept my apologies!

My sincere thanks also to Epaminondas Argyropoulos, the architect of the house of Josephine who designed it as if he had seen it with his own eyes!

As well as to Kostas Sofikitis, the radio operator who lent me some of his specialized knowledge on wireless transmission.

Thanks also... to those who helped me when I waved my arms around and lost all semblance of calmness... They know who they are... Marie Nakou of "word" and Chrisoula Palla of "quark"...

Thanks, OF COURSE, also go to my Publisher, that trusted me and did so many indulgent favours to me... and to all the team of Cambridge Pen, thank you for doing such great job...

Acknowledgements

While special thanks go to Katherina Papathanassiou for drawing the very best out of the story, treating the manuscript along with me with such understanding and respect.

Above all, thanks to my family, who were there before the book and will be there long after it, and who often forced to exit in total silence, so as to avoid interrupting my train of thoughts and all these on...

Last but not least, thanks to all of you, who are reading this book right now...

Lily

P.S. I have even some written pages in my drawer and even some ideas on my mind...

www.ingramcontent.com/pod-product-compliance
Lightning Source LLC
Chambersburg PA
CBHW022103090426
42743CB00008B/706

9781905399987